BI 0561651 4

KU-490-366

Life and Death of
the Schools Council

CITY OF BIRMINGHAM
POLYTECHNIC LIBRARY

AUTHOR

TITLE   Life & death of the schools council

SUBJECT No. 379.15/Pla

BOOK No.   05616514

P53178-B1(C)

This book is a celebration of the work of the Schools Council, a tribute to all those who were involved in and who supported it during twenty distinguished years, and an indictment of those who did it malicious damage.

Life and Death of the Schools Council

Edited by
Maurice Plaskow

The Falmer Press

A member of the Taylor & Francis Group
London and Philadelphia

CITY OF BIRMINGHAM
LIBRARY
POLYTECHNIC

UK   The Falmer Press, Falmer House, Barcombe, Lewes, East Sussex, BN8 5DL

USA   The Falmer Press, Taylor & Francis Inc., 242 Cherry Street, Philadelphia, PA 19106-1906

Copyright © Selection and editorial material M. Plaskow 1985

All rights reserved. No part of this publication may be reproduced, stored in a retrieval system, or transmitted in any form or by any means, electronic, mechanical, photocopying, recording or otherwise, without permission in writing from the Publisher.

First published 1985

CITY OF BIRMINGHAM
POLYTECHNIC LIBRARY

BOOK
No.   05616514

SUBJECT
No. 379·15 Pla

Library of Congress Cataloging in Publication Data

Main entry under title:

Life and death of the schools council.

Includes indexes.
   1. Schools council (Great Britain)—History—
Addresses, essays, lectures. 2. Curriculum planning—
Great Britain—History—Addresses, essays, lectures.
I. Plaskow, Maurice.
LB2901.L54 1985 375′.001′0941 84-28644
ISBN 0-85000-058-1
ISBN 0-85000-057-3 (pbk.)

Typeset in 11/13 Garamond by
Imago Publishing Ltd, Thame, Oxon.

Jacket design by Leonard Williams

Printed in Great Britain by Taylor & Francis (Printers) Ltd, Basingstoke

Contents

Contents

Schools Council Officers 1964–1981

Chairmen

SIR JOHN MAUD	1964–66
MR ALAN (LATER LORD) BULLOCK	1966–69
DAME MURIEL STEWART	1969–72
SIR LINCOLN RALPHS	1972–75
SIR ALEX SMITH	1975–78
MR JOHN TOMLINSON	1978–81
DR PETER ANDREWS (acting chairman)	1982
MR ARNOLD JENNINGS (acting chairman)	1983–84

Joint Secretaries

D.H. Morrell (1964–66)	(DES)
R.W. Morris (1964–66)	(Inspectorate)
G.K. Caston (1966–70)	(DES)
J.G. Owen (1966–68)	(Somerset LEA)
R. Sibson (1966–73)	(Inspectorate)
Professor J. Wrigley (1966–75) (Appointed as Director of Studies and Professor of Curriculum Research and Development)	(Reading University)
G.A. Rogers (1968–70)	(Inner London Education Authority)
G.W. Cooksey (1970–73)	(Derbyshire LEA; Shirebrook School)
G.F. Cockerill (1970–73)	(DES)
V.H. Stevens (1973–76)	(DES)
A.J. Light (1973–75)	(Bristol LEA)
Dr J. Stroud (1973–76)	(King Edward VI Grammar School, Southampton).
J.G. Raitt (1976–79)	(West Sussex LEA)

Schools Council Officers 1964–1981

P.M. Dines (1976–79)   (Cramlington High School).
Mrs D.M. White (1977–78)   (DES)

Secretary
J.F. Mann (1979–83)   (Sheffield LEA)

Deputy Secretary
K. McWilliams (1980–83)
In December 1983 appointed
Chief Executive.

Chronology

1964 (March)	Lockwood Report recommends new body for curriculum and examinations
(1 October)	Schools Council for Curriculum and Examinations set up
1965	CSE held for first time
1965–67	Enquiry undertaken into attitudes of pupils, former pupils, parents and teachers towards schooling
1966	First Constitutional Review Working Party
1968	First (16+) and second (post 16+) examination committees established
(March)	Schools Council and Standing Conference on University Entrance (SCUE) agree to set up working party to study possibility of reform of sixth form curriculum and examinations
(November)	First meeting of Working Party on Pupils' Records: record keeping in primary schools and transfer of information to secondary
(December)	New constitution adopted establishing Programme Committee as senior educational policy committee with teacher majority
1969 (January)	Schools Council registered as a charity
	Three national conferences on *Teachers' Centres and the Changing Curriculum*

(May)	Setting up of working parties on Gifted Children in Primary Schools, and the Needs of Handicapped Pupils
(December)	Joint statement by first and second sixth form working parties: proposals for the curriculum and examinations in the sixth form (Q and F)
1970 (1 April)	Schools Council becomes independent of the Department of Education and Science
	First five humanities project packs of material published
(July)	Recommendation 'that there should be a single examination system at the age of 16+'
	Working party on the 13–16 curriculum set up
1971	Secretary of State for Education, Mrs Margaret Thatcher, visited the Council twice
(June)	Joint Examinations Sub-committee (JESC) set up
(September)	Central Examinations Research and Development Unit (CERDU) set up
(October)	Exams Bulletin 23 published: *Common System of Examining at 16+*
1972 (January)	Proposals for Certificate of Extended Education (CEE)
(March)	Dissemination Working Party set up
1973 (March)	Margaret Thatcher addresses Governing Council
(July)	Proposal for official grading scheme at 'O' level
(October)	Dissemination Working Party report received
(November)	First regional information centre opened in Newcastle
1974	Secretary of State for Education, Mr Reg Prentice, addresses Governing Council
1975 (January)	16 syllabus groups for N and F established
	Programme Committee approved principle of local curriculum development support

	Report of 13–16 curriculum working party published
	Aims of Primary Education published
(July)	Constitutional Review Working Party submitted new proposals
	New 'O' level grading scheme implemented
1976	Proposals for single system at 16+, and CEE (17+) submitted to Secretary of State
	Appearance of 'Yellow Paper' accusing the Council of mediocre work
1977 (January)	Constitutional Review Working Party established
(March)	Secretary of State sets up steering group to investigate further single system at 16+ (Waddell Committee)
(November)	Secretary of State sets up steering committee to review CEE pilot schemes (Keohane Committee)
	Industry project started work
	N and F pilot studies published
1978	New constitution accepted: September — first meeting of Professional Committee November — first meeting of Convocation
(September)	Joint project with the Open University, Evaluation and the Teacher
	First report of *Impact and Take-up* enquiry
	Appointment of Council's first Permanent Secretary, John Mann
1979 (July)	Publication of *Principles and Programmes*, setting out priorities
	Decision by Secretary of State to retain 'A' levels
1980	Four programmes of work begin
	Industry project interim report published

		Proposal for 'I' level exam (intermediate, between 'O' and 'A' levels)
		Secretary of State accepts principle of single system at 16+
1981	(March)	Independent review of the Council set up under Nancy Trenaman
		Publication of *Practical Curriculum*
	(April)	Secondary Science Curriculum Review Established
	(October)	Nancy Trenaman recommends that the Schools Council should continue
1982	(April)	Secretary of State, Sir Keith Joseph, announces intention to disband the Schools Council
1983	(March)	Secondary Examinations Council (SEC) set up
	(August)	SEC and the Council move to Newcombe House, Notting Hill
	(October)	*Primary Practice* published
	(November)	Membership of the new Schools Curriculum Development Committee (SCDC) announced
1984	(January)	All Schools Council staff declared redundant
		First meeting of SCDC
	(31 March)	*Schools Council closes*

The Life and Death of the Schools Council — A Long View from the Inside

Maurice Plaskow

The Schools Council was conceived as a hopeful act of reconciliation between central and local government and teachers. It was born into a time of growth and optimism. It survived twenty years of challenge and turbulence to promising adulthood, before Sir Keith Joseph decided on its closure.

The chapters which follow are personal accounts by people who were closely involved with the Council from conception to execution. Together they offer an unusual collection of contemporary history, both educational and political. The period 1964–84 spans dramatic change and development, as the whole system underwent reorganisation and appraisal. And the world of education mirrored the uncertainties, the losses of familiar landmarks, the upheaval of accepted values which disrupted society in general.

Anyone who imagines, or plaintively urges that education has nothing to do with politics has to be simple-minded. The investment of a large chunk of national resources into a compulsory and comprehensive education system is a political act. It is based on certain beliefs, assumptions, values and expectations. Over the past twenty years many of these have been called into question. The work of the Schools Council itself contributed to opening out the discussion, raising issues in public which previously had been confined to limited, usually academic circles, since no wider forum existed for engaging a broad, democratic constituency.

I joined the headquarters staff of the Council at Great Portland Street in 1970, at the point when it had become an independent charity. My association with the Council began three years earlier, when I joined the Humanities Curriculum Project team, directed by Lawrence Stenhouse. I was present at most of the meetings of the major policy committees, and at their regular residential policy reviews, right up to January 1984, when staff were declared redundant and the decision to close was finally implemented.

It was an exhilarating, if often frustrating experience. The atmosphere within the Council was at all times congenial; there was a deep sense of purpose: a feeling that the work of projects, in particular, was making a significant and lasting impact upon educational thinking. I have no doubt that the level of curriculum discourse over the time when I knew the Council rose substantially, in no small measure due to the fact that curriculum development had become a growth industry, and a great many teachers had become aware both of the need, and of their professional responsibility, to respond sensitively and conscientiously to issues of curriculum construction, content and pedagogy, evaluation and assessment.

In the years following the publication of the *Practical Curriculum* in 1981 it was enormously heartening, going round the country, meeting teachers, advisers and often parents and employers, to find how ready they all were to confront the complex problems facing schools, and that they were looking to the Council for leadership and guidance. Others in this book speculate that this may well have been a contributory reason for the closure; there was a possibility of a shift in the balance of influence, if not power, over the curriculum, at a time when it became increasingly clear that government intended to adopt a strongly interventionist stance on what should be taught in our schools.

Structure and Politics

Given the representative nature of the Council it was inevitable that it should be a political institution. What was remarkable was that, on the whole, it worked through consensus not conflict. It was the only forum where all the educational bodies met, on neutral territory, to discuss matters concerning the curriculum, rather than salaries, conditions of service and professional policy.

Although this sometimes inevitably meant that decisions were taken at the level of the lowest common denominator of agreement, it is salutary to reflect on the sensible nature of most of those decisions, and on the number of adventurous and imaginative projects which were funded. The teachers, more often than not, agreed with each other on policy issues. If they dominated Programme Committee in the 1970s, until the constitutional review, it was as much because the Local Education Authorities (LEA) and Department of Education and Science (DES) didn't get their acts together and develop an alternative policy. Of course the National Union of Teachers (NUT) group was powerful: it was large and articulate, well serviced by its officers, so that the representatives came to meetings fully briefed.

But more than the groups, key individuals played a role during those years which profoundly and consistently influenced the course of events.[1] Sheila Wood, then of the Assistant Mistresses Association, invariably came to meetings well prepared; one of the few people who could be relied upon to have carefully read the papers, her interventions, often early in the discussions, were powerful, positive and informed. She was respected and difficult to resist. Proposers had to work very hard to retrieve any issue against which she had spoken firmly.

Arnold Jennings and Max Morris were also long-serving Council members of considerable influence and, although they didn't get their way as often as Sheila Wood, the three of them made enormous contributions, especially within the Examinations Committee. It was ironic that Arnold Jennings was Acting Chairman faced with the depressing task of seeing the Council out.

The other outstanding figure, in terms of respect and influence, was Ron Cocking of the National Association of Schoolmasters/Union of Women Teachers (NAS/UWT). His tragically early death deprived the Council of a strong supporter. His continued presence may well have made a difference to the Council's outcome.

The fact that these four individuals had different constituencies underlines how oversimple the view is of NUT control of the Council, or even of a teacher conspiracy. If teachers had the major influence in Council policy during the 1970s it was because they brought greater commitment to its work, and the other groups did not appear to object strongly to the general direction and particular decisions.

The role played by DES officials and Her Majesty's Inspectorate (HMI) was always enigmatic, and must be returned to. There was very little continuity of representation of DES personnel, and few of them understood the nature of curriculum development anyway. HMI were strangely reticent in policy committees, although many of them were helpful and supportive in subject committees. It was only when the notorious Yellow Book appeared in 1976 that the real views (unsupported by evidence) of those in the DES surfaced. From that time the signals indicating hostility to the Council were clear, and it was naively negligent of the rest of the Council, including the staff, not to have recognized the danger and done more to secure its position (a point made by Christopher Price).

Perhaps the Council paid the price of an untidily democratic institution. Its procedures were heavily bureaucratic and arcane, and until the development of *Principles and Programmes* (see the chapter by Don Cooper) there was no coherent policy about the curriculum. Response to proposals from external sources was either instant death, or what must have felt like a long process of attrition to those who sometimes had to wait eighteen months or so for a final judgment, as papers trundled through committees. It was not unknown for proposers to appear and argue their case before six different groups, all of whom then expressed a view to Programme Committee, who gave the final verdict.

Structure and Staff

The position of staff in all this was complex and subtle, and changed interestingly over time.

The immensely important contribution of Derek Morrell is well-documented. He set a vision for the Council which remained, at various degrees of brightness, until its death. Geoffrey Caston continued the campaigning, buccaneering style. In that early period 1964–70, there is little doubt that the joint secretaries created and built on a sense of creative excitement which led to the funding of some of the Council's major projects, in English, science and technology, and the Raising of the School Leaving Age (RoSLA) RoSLA programme of which the Humanities Project and Geography for the Young School Leaver (GYSL) were a part.

The underlying values and concerns of these initiatives were remarkably in tune with the motivation behind the events of 1968. The ethos can be summarized by the title which Lawrence Stenhouse gave to an article which he wrote about The Humanities Curriculum Project (HCP) which appeared in *Dialogue* 5 (then the Schools Council's journal), in which he set out the necessary conditions for giving reality to the slogan 'Secondary education for All':

> We need to establish a new climate of relationships with adolescents which takes account of their responsibility and is not authoritarian. Education must be founded on their coopera-tion, not on coercion. We must find a way of expressing our common humanity with our pupils, and we must be sensitive to the need to justify the decisions of authority to those affected by

them. At the same time we need gradually to develop the capacity for independent study and enquiry with the flexibility of mind which this implies. In short, we need to transform our adolescent pupils into students.

Although the majority of Council staff came on a short-term basis, they were quickly affected by the atmosphere of the place, and the enthusiasm to make things happen, to bring about constructive change. The friendly, supportive climate was greatly helped by a splendid civil servant, an administrative officer, Ann George. She was in the marvellous tradition of someone who had left school early, entered the post office, and made her way up the service by merit and integrity. Her stories about her early experiences were endlessly enthralling. The Council owed her much, and we were all deeply saddened at her death, not very long after her retirement.

In the early years of the Council there were more seconded civil servants than directly recruited staff. They ranged from assistant secretaries who did a stint as one of the three joint secretaries; specialist HMI (two of the early joint secretaries also came from the ranks of senior HMI); professional staff who acted as project and then curriculum officers; and a greater number of support staff who brought a variety of administrative experience and ensured the efficient running of the Council.

Some of the civil servants did not take to the less structured, informal style of the Council. Many more of them enjoyed their stay, and often returned to Elizabeth House reluctantly, because their career advancement lay there.

Within the DES there is, therefore, a considerable number of people with direct experience of the Schools Council, who could have provided first hand evidence to those who preferred to rely on rumour and prejudice about the work of the Council and its quality.

As some of the contributors point out, those senior DES officials who seemed particularly hostile to the Council knew least about it from their own contact. They found the open, and at times vigorous, discussions abrasive and difficult to control: people actually seemed to care about issues more than neat procedures. I was cautioned by one civil servant joint secretary about becoming too involved with projects; it would cloud my judgment and endanger my loyalty.

In the last three years the number of civil servants declined to a very small number, and they almost completely disappeared in the final months. HMI had ceased to be seconded for some years. Links with DES became more formal and fragile, and while their representatives were party to all the working groups and committees, there had never been reciprocity. We had very good relationships with many HMI, who gave valuable advice. But always there was an arms-length feel; sentences were prefaced with please-don't-quote-me; or concluded with, please-don't-minute-that. None of the HMI approached to contribute to this collection was prepared to do so.

Democratic institutions need to be comprehensive and convivial if they are to remain buoyant, and not drown. Many hundreds of men and women from different sectors participated in the Council's work. It was time-consuming, devouring forests, patience-trying and over-elaborate. But it was evolving: the 1978 constitution was a remarkable achievement in realizing a new alignment, in which the teachers recognized the place of the paymasters and gave up their in-built majorities. And part of the demonstration of the new confidence and trust was a readiness to allow staff a more equal role in policy and planning. The move to programmes instead of projects gave staff power as well as influence, and promoted them from functionaries. The system of monitoring groups brought together members and staff in a working relationship which had not previously existed. The production of the *Practical Curriculum, Primary Practice*, and other documents of the Council's last years were testimony to a partnership which promised well for the future. It may be immodest fancy to suggest that the likelihood of positive leadership was one of the real, if unspoken factors in the Council's demise. John Tomlinson records how the Council was asked to delay publication of the *Practical Curriculum* so that the DES could publish their *School Curriculum* document first.

The Rhetoric and the Reality

With the agreement on *Principles and Programmes* the Council for the first time had an articulated policy, an agenda for action. It may have contained the whole of educational life, but in practice some focus was emerging, and there is no doubt that in a second phase there would have been more coherence and concentration.

Except for the RoSLA programme the Council's stance was essentially responsive to external proposals in its first phase. There is a frail pattern to be detected in retrospect, but like examination criteria, on the whole the judgments came from the collective experience of the committees. Their reasons were never available for public scrutiny. The impressive thing is how many outstanding projects were supported. In some cases the members could not have predicted the outcomes from the original submissions. But the body of work is a tribute to the backing given to innovatory flair, to quality of imagination and experiment.

The inventory of projects is outstanding by any reckoning, and gained wide international recognition. Much of the material was translated. The roll call contains some of the most respected names in curriculum development. Indeed, the Council was the major training ground for curriculum developers and evaluators, many of whom occupy senior positions both in the UK and around the world.

Possibly the Council itself never fully understood the breadth and quality of its products. By Council here I mean members, whose contact with the work was inevitably at a distance, and fragmentary. One of the identity problems always was 'who spoke for, and represented the Council.'

Because the rhetoric stressed that the Council was there to 'offer greater choice to teachers' there was an inevitable dilemma about achieving maximum impact and penetration within the system. The constitution enshrined the general principle 'that each school should have the fullest possible measure of responsibility for its own work, with its own curriculum and teaching methods based on the needs of its own pupils and evolved by its own staff.'

Added to this was the agreement with educational publishers that material would be put out to tender and handled through their network. Once published, projects took their chance in the marketplace. I remember Harry Rée suggesting in committee that, if the Council had confidence in its work it should promote it. It was as though he had uttered an obscene heresy. Foreign visitors could never understand the quaint English perversity in setting up a national agency, supported by the whole of the education service, which pretended that its curriculum offerings, painstakingly developed and carefully piloted by teachers, had not greater authority or credence than any textbook.

There were other unresolved paradoxes, especially the Council's relationship with teacher training agencies. As early as the annual report for 1968/69, after its first constitutional review, the Council stated that projects should include an in-service training element. 'But, this apart, the Council would not provide in-service training itself nor act as a coordinating body.' Projects recognized within a short time that there could be no curriculum development without the involvement and understanding of teachers. Nor would it become part of a teacher's expectation and repertoire unless there had been some introduction and familiarization at initial training. There were increasing links made with colleges of education; and of course the Council had been largely instrumental in encouraging the growth of teachers' centres. But the relationships were never fully worked out or completely satisfactory; not least because of the constant turmoil in which institutions found themselves over the same period. It is an interesting irony that the problem was recognized by Margaret Thatcher when she was Secretary of State for Education — one of the few Secretaries of State to visit the Council[2] — and she referred to it when she addressed the Governing Council in March 1973: 'it is vital that those who train teachers should be familiar with the work of the Schools Council' she said. Ten years is a very long time in politics.

Curriculum and Examinations

Undoubtedly the biggest unresolved issue on the Council's agenda was the nature and role of the examination system, and its relationship with the curriculum.

Again the slogan was impeccable: examinations exist to serve the curriculum. It just didn't appear to work out that way; indeed, the testimony of many teachers was that exactly the reverse was true. The conflicts and the agony about exams throughout its life throws into relief the difficulty which we (the country) have had in constructing secondary education for all, within a comprehensive system, which also tried to work out the implications of those other slogans, like democratic pluralism; equality of opportunity; cultural diversity.

One has to go back to the inherited context. 1963, when the creation of the Schools Council was announced, saw the appearance of the Newsom Report, *Half Our Future*. In 1964 came the commitment to raising the school leaving age (at that time to be 1970/71), which gave RoSLA to our vocabulary. 1965 brought from the succeeding Labour government the notorious Crosland circular 10/65, which heralded secondary reorganization on comprehensive lines, sold to the middle classes as grammar schools for all.

CSE already existed as a sub 'O' level certificate to help raise morale in the secondary modern schools. Now all students were to remain in compulsory education until 16, when they could be presented for public examinations.

It was inevitable that the Council should mount a major programme to help teachers prepare for RoSLA. However, the thinking was still within the Newsom framework, that the less (academically) able and alienated students required a differentiated curriculum, which might provide a more integrated programme than the traditional single subject 'O' level route. In fact, the projects which emerged, HCP, GYSL Moral Education, Maths for the Majority, seized the opportunity for more fundamental curriculum thinking, in terms of content, approach, values and attitudes. There is a remarkable similarity in underlying principles.

Until the cold winds of the mid-1970s froze the optimism the vogue words were autonomy, independence, participation, process, to be achieved through a more open pedagogy which gave students greater responsibility for their own learning. History 13–16 developed this approach very successfully presenting history as detection and reconstruction, rather than a collection of unrelated nuggets of information to be memorized. History 13–16 negotiated an 'O' level with an examining board in order to gain a legitimate place in the curriculum. Even HCP recognized the reality of examination pressure and, while it did not advocate or construct an examination, said that the team would advise any school which wished to produce an examination which would not damage the integrity of the project.

All these initiatives were an attempt to reduce the divisiveness within the bipartite system. If there were notions of educational worthwhileness which should inform the structure of the educational experience during compulsory schooling, then access should be provided to everyone. The teacher's task, as Bruner had suggested, was in finding the appropriate strategies for enabling students to gain a confident hold on a central body of knowledge and skills and understandings which would, in the eloquent words of the Warnock Report 'enable them to enter the world after formal education is over as active participants in society and responsible contributors to it.'

The clamour for accountability, crudely equated with pressures for cost-effectiveness, has produced again attempts to create not just criteria of value, but measures for assessment. The turbulence in the economic system in the mid-1970s, the decline of traditional industry and dramatic competition in new high-tech industries understandably set off panic reactions and authoritarian solutions. The last ten years have not been a happy time for education, and it should not be surprising that the Schools Council did not escape from the general thrashing.

The Final Years

Increasingly through the 1970s the Council's committees and officers became enervated by the cumbersome procedures, and disappointed that an institution in the change business seemed to find itself unable to learn easily from its experience.

The infamous Yellow Book of 1976, which provided the briefing for James Callaghan's Ruskin's speech in which he berated education for failing to respond to the changing national needs, hastened the Council's resolve to undertake a review of its ways of working — before someone else did it for them.

The 1978 constitution which emerged was a remarkable accommodation, which considerably widened the Council's constituency, and was a masterly and imaginative achievement of Sir Alex Smith as Chairman in moving the Council nearer to an educational parliament, in which teachers still had a centrally acknowledged, if not longer paramount, position. Staff, privately, considered the changes a step towards a further phase which would reduce further the unwieldy nature of Professional Committee, in particular, and forge closer working links between staff and members.

The Monitoring Groups of the programmes were an interesting experimental start in this process, and brought about at once greater central control of the development work, and a more cooperative, trusting relationship between staff and committee members — and indeed HMI and DES staff.

But alas, too late. The impression in the minds of some influential politicians now in government that the Council was both subversive and ineffectual, was shared by some of the senior DES officials, who had least direct experience of the Council and its work. In 1981 an independent enquiry into the Council under Mrs. Nancy Trenaman was set up, within the general 'quango hunt'. With no background and commitment to the Council she reported in the autumn of that year that it should not only continue but, that if it didn't exist, it would need to be invented.

This clearly wasn't the hoped-for message. It took six months for a response to emerge from the DES. In April 1982 Sir Keith Joseph announced in the House of Commons that he intended to disband the Council. Despite the protests and the difficulty in understanding the logic of establishing two separate bodies, one for examinations and the other for curriculum, the intention was carried out, albeit with an inefficiency which would have been comical had it not been so serious both for the professional careers of staff, and the damage to the carefully built up network of teachers and others in the localities.

The process of run-down took two years. The Council had itself proposed a move as an economy gesture, which had been blocked by the DES because of the uncertain future. In the event the move took place, several months later than planned, and therefore at far greater cost. Every time the DES held up negotiations or opposed action plans put forward by the Council management, they had to return at a later date and concede. The terms on which staff were eventually released, while not ungenerous, had to be wrung from a reluctant DES, with threats of legal action. Redundancy and compensation payments were, in the end, larger than would have been the case had the DES accepted the proposals put forward at the outset by the staff union. Enormous amounts of time and energy had to be spent in producing papers which patiently explained to the DES why their arguments were flawed and their proposals untenable. The whole episode was a study in how not to conduct negotiations, and caused great distress and anxiety to many people who had given loyal service to the Council, and who believed in its work.

What of the Future?

This has not been an attempt to be scholarly or definitive. There is much to be written about individual projects, about the process of change, about strategies of innovation, about the paradox of central bodies within a decentralized system.

The marvellous thing was that the Council existed at all, survived twenty fascinating years, and was poised to consolidate itself within the fabric of a fiercely independent system. I suspect that, had it continued, the process of agreed development would have gone faster and more purposefully forward. The trust had been created, people were huddling together out of the cold, the credentials were sufficiently accepted to take some risk for common preservation.

Democratic pluralism cannot be reconciled with authoritarian dogma. Either we achieve some value consensus within a workable framework, or we must become resigned to central direction, prescription through authority, with minimal decoration at the margins. The major thrust of the Council's activities in its last years was directed at increasing teachers' professionalism, and giving guidance to schools on how they might develop more effective self-evaluating procedures. This could create the confidence within which schools would more readily open themselves both to public scrutiny and discussion about their tasks. In the long term it would be a more hopeful approach than the imposition of external constraints, whether in the form of a national curriculum, or governing boards with majorities of parents charged with curriculum control. That is perhaps an insidious device for slowing down the rate of innovation aimed at meeting the challenge of changing needs, and together with initiatives designed to introduce a more heavily pre-vocational curriculum, could point back to the elementary, rather than forward to a comprehensive tradition.

I would want to leave the last words to Lawrence Stenhouse, as a tribute to the outstanding contribution he made to an understanding of the curriculum development process, and what it could mean to a new concept of both curriculum and the teacher.

That was the title of one of the last public lectures he gave, at Goldsmiths' College in 1982, and he ended it with an eloquent, and more overtly political warning than was usual in his talks:

> Our system of public education is notable for being in the power of those who do not commit their own children to it and it is accordingly vulnerable. The powerful still do not favour the cultivation among the lower orders of the scepticism and critical intelligence that is valued among their betters. It is for that reason that they point backwards to basics in the face of the potential of the exciting curricula in literacy and numeracy and knowledge to be found in the recent curriculum movement, in the leading state schools and in the more enlightened private schools.
>
> The decline in investment and support for public education in this country at the moment is at many points a vindictive, rather than a prudent, economy. At stake is more than a hundred years of adventure beyond the mere basics, a span in which schools — fitfully no doubt — have tried to make people independent thinkers capable of participation in the democratic process and of deciding what the future of their own society shall be like. Perhaps a faith in expansion and progress underlay that provision for the citizen. We must now find ways of ensuring that a defensive, and more apprehensive, establishment in the context of a contracting economy does not make a critical education an education reserved for privilege.

Notes

1 The importance of these powerful personalities must not be under-rated. I vividly remember the occasion when a proposal went to Programme Committee with the incautious title 'Graphicacy'. (the development of visual awareness and understanding). The doyen of the LEA representatives, now a noble Lord, intervened with: 'what will it be next: lunacy, I suppose?' End of discussion.

2 On her tour she went round the exhibition of material, and read the panel on the Humanities Project. Her terse comment was: "when I was a girl, I was taught to know the difference between right and wrong".

Out of the Secret Garden

Arnold Jennings

I have been asked to write on three topics, the setting up of the Council, the relations between its examinations work and its curriculum work, and the experience of 'presiding over the obsequies'. These might seem quite separate and distinct, but they are different aspects or periods of the Council's basic task and aim, bringing about by the consent of those concerned change in the curriculum. I would like to add some remarks on a fourth, also related — the future of the Council.

The Setting-up of the Council

During the post-war period of rapid educational development of the most wide-ranging kind, a number of people in the Ministry of Education came to the view that the Ministry's traditional position of standing outside curriculum matters and even of public debate on curriculum was a hindrance to it in dealing with many of the problems that faced it. One story says that Sir David Eccles was dismayed to find at international conferences on education that when asked questions about school curricula he was unable to provide any clear answer. This is probably personalising a general view in the Ministry; but Eccles was the Minister who first decided it was time to change this position, and announced his decision. In a debate in the Commons on the Crowther Report in March 1960 he originated the phrase 'the secret garden of the curriculum', and said that Parliamentary debates on education should not be only about bricks and mortar and organisation, but should include discussion on what was being taught in the schools. In future he would 'try to make the Ministry's voice' (notice, not 'the Minister's') heard rather more often and positively and no doubt more controversially'. To do this the Ministry would need to carry out more research of its own and to collect more statistics (both recommended by Crowther); this was being undertaken.

A new section was formed in the Ministry of Education to carry out this task. It was a small group, including HMIs administrators and 'appropriate experts' brought in from outside the Ministry. Professor Jack Wrigley, who was brought in as such an expert, has said that he was in fact the only one brought in from outside the Ministry of Education. It was called the Curriculum Study Group. It was established in February 1962, almost two years after Eccles' announcement in the Commons. It has been said that the delay was because of divisions of opinion among the HMIs; some might think such a timescale of action from the Ministry of Education calls for no particular explanation.

When it was being set up, this was treated as an internal matter for the Ministry of Education in that no consultation of any kind with the various educational interests took place. After it had been set up, the Permanent Secretary wrote a circular letter to the educational associations, in which he said that 'the Ministry and the Inspectorate have a useful contribution to make to thinking about the educational process', and this could take the form of 'placing before our partners in the educational service a range of possible solutions to future problems'.

All this sent shock waves reverberating through the educational world. The doctrine of the decentralization of power in public education, chiefly between the Ministry, the LEAs and the teachers, as the corner-stone of freedom of thought and of action in English education was generally accepted, and hitherto it had been taken for granted that the Ministry accepted it too. The great fear was that this was the not very thin end of a rather obvious wedge, and that in the end the Ministry would impose central control of the curriculum. It was taken for granted that that was anathema, because it would be destructive of those freedoms of thought and action in the curriculum field. Professor Wrigley says 'One headmaster wrote "Have we fought two world wars for this?"'[1] Sir William Alexander for the LEAs and Sir Ronald Gould for the teachers both saw the Curriculum Study Group as a major threat to English liberties.

If the Ministry's 'voice' was 'heard', 'placing possible solutions before our partners', for how long would those partners be free to decline the offered advice, and reject the solution 'placed before them', if they came to the conclusion that something else was a better answer? The head of the Curriculum Studies Group was Derek Morrell, a civil servant marked out as a high flier. He had registered a success in

Buildings branch, in which LEAs notably found they could not do what they wanted if Buildings Branch strongly disagreed. School building costs had been successfully reduced, inter alia by cutting the amount of floor space other than classroom space — which often simply meant permanent congestion in the corridors between lessons. The LEAs knew this, but were not allowed to alter the plans. So they, as well as the teachers, were not encouraged, and felt profoundly suspicious of the Curriculum Study Group.

The Secondary Schools Examinations Council (SSEC) was a body, which would now be called a quango', set up in 1917 by the Board of Education when it established the School Certificate and the Higher School Certificate. The Board undertook 'to perform the functions of a coordinating authority for secondary school examinations', and it set up the SSEC, to whom it delegated all the day-to-day work in this function, and also invited it to offer advice to the Board from time to time on possible improvements in the examinations, 'especially to keep the examinations in touch with the development of new studies and methods in the schools'.

In the first post-war decade the school leaving age went up to 15, and the secondary modern school developed rapidly in many directions. Many of these schools, and their pupils and their parents, thirsted for examination success and certificates. Not many of them could achieve this at GCE 'O' level, which had been designed with different candidates in mind, but there was no other 'official' school examination. Supply rapidly arose to meet demand, and all manner of independent examinations of varying credibility, standing and authorization were soon attracting volume entries.

In July 1958 the SSEC set up a committee under Robert Beloe, then Chief Education Officer for Surrey, to consider this situation and make recommendations. Its report,[2] in July 1960, recommended the introduction of what is now the CSE, and laid down its main principles. The SSEC recommended its adoption, and in July 1961 Sir David Eccles accepted their recommendation and took the decision to introduce the CSE. He asked the SSEC to draft the outlines of the new examination far enough for it to be set up. An obvious handicap to the SSEC in doing this, which diminished their authority considerably, was that the SSEC had been constituted to deal with the School Certificate, the Higher School Certificate and GCE 'O' and 'A' levels, and consisted of people who knew about GCE, grammar schools, sixth-forms and universities, but was notably short on people who knew what a secondary modern school was like.

Eccles added some new members to the SSEC to strengthen it on this side. But even then its CSE Standing Committee-whose recommendations for the setting up of the CSE[3] were duly published in August 1962 — consisted of fifteen of the previous members of the SSEC, two of whom were serving heads of secondary moderns, one who had been, one head of a secondary technical and one of a comprehensive, and one Chief Education Officer; to these they coopted a secondary modern head and a secondary technical head — which still left more than half the Committee consisting of people with little or no real knowledge of the schools they were legislating for. This was neither a satisfactory nor a defensible position, and demands were quickly voiced for the SSEC's constitution to be amended and its membership further enlarged so as to accommodate its new sphere of interest.

The Schools Council

At this stage Derek Morrell, the Secretary of the Curriculum Study Group, produced four brilliant ideas —

1   In order to disarm suspicion of the Curriculum Study Group and enable it to go ahead and do its work unhampered by this, to take the Curriculum Study Group right out of the Ministry of Education, and to put it under the control of a body representing all the major educational interests, and so constituted that neither the Ministry nor the LEAs could control it. I do not remember, and have not been able to find out, whether this was an original idea of Morrell's, or one that had been put forward by Alexander and/or Gould which he adopted. It was referred to in the Lockwood Report as 'the Minister's proposal'.

2   To widen further the membership of the SSEC, and to make this too an undeniably fully representative body.

3   The master-stroke — to put both the Curriculum Study Group and the SSEC into one body, which would have responsibility for the functions of both.

4   The most daring — to state as part of the constitution of the new body

    (a)   that curriculum should come first, and examinations follow it, and not, as normally happened, the other way round.

(b)   that the new body should have one of its elements in a guaranteed majority, and that should be the teachers. This was to guarantee that neither the Ministry nor the LEAs could, through the new body, force curriculum innovations on to an unwilling teaching profession. It was also in pursuance of the stated aim that each school should be responsible for its own curriculum and teaching methods, evolved by itself to meet the needs of its pupils.

This last idea was also not plucked out of the air, but already had a longer and more conventionally respectable history than is often realized or now remembered. To quote only from Government publications, the Spens Report[4] in 1938 said 'there can be little doubt that in many Secondary Schools the (School) Certificate examination is now the dominant factor in determining the curriculum for the majority of the pupils below the age of 16'. It quoted the Board of Education Circular 1034 of March 1918, which laid down as 'a cardinal principle that the examination should follow the curriculum and not determine it', and added 'in practice this principle has been reversed'. The Spens Report also said 'in several important aspects the influence of the examination and the process of preparation for it are inimical to the healthy growth in mind and body of a large number of children who pass through the Grammar School', and 'observing how completely and exclusively the State may occupy the field (of education), turning the schools and the teachers into mere instruments of its policies, vehicles for the dissemination of the ideas it approves ... we assert our faith in the English compromise between State regulation and freedom of teaching', and concluded 'we desire to leave as much freedom as possible to schools in the selection of studies and in their content'. The Norwood Report[5] in 1943 said 'there should be freedom to schools to devise curricula suited to their pupils and to local needs' and 'examinations should be a sub-ordinate part in the school economy'; 'the examination is best conducted by the teachers themselves as being those who should know their pupils' work and ought therefore to be those best able to form a judgment on it', and (Recommendation 9) 'change in the examination entirely internal, that is to say, conducted by the teachers at the school on syllabuses and papers framed by themselves'.

These ideas of Derek Morrell's were given immediate backing by Sir Edward Boyle as Minister of Education. He called a representative meeting under his own chairmanship in July 1963, which appointed the Lockwood Working Party 'to examine the lines on which action might be taken'. Do not underestimate the importance of 'called a representative meeting, which appointed', as distinct from 'he appointed'. The Lockwood Committee reported in March 1964[6] with clear recommendations for the setting up of a body to provide 'new cooperative machinery in the fields of the schools' curricula and examinations' to be called 'The Schools Council for the Curriculum and Examinations' which should be a fully representative body 'including representatives of all the interests principally concerned', and gave a detailed constitution for it (which Professor Wrigley[7] has told us he remembers Derek Morrell writing in his room at the Ministry of Education). The first of the seventeen recommendations embodying this was:

> We reaffirm the importance of the principle that the schools should have the fullest possible measure of responsibility for their own work, including responsibility for their own curricula and teaching methods, which should be evolved by their own staff to meet the needs of their own pupils. We believe however that positive action is needed to uphold this principle'.

The principle is stated in full three times in the fourteen pages of the Lockwood Report, in the first instance in the words 'We noted that it has along been accepted in England and Wales that the schools should have the fullest possible measure. To this they added 'The present arrangements for determining the curriculum in schools and the related examinations are not working well: in particular teachers have insufficient scope for making or recommending modifications in the curriculum and examinations', and that there was 'insufficient coordination' between curriculum and teaching methods and examinations, and between entry requirements to higher and further education and the work of the schools. Schools 'consider, in our view rightly, that the underlying trend is towards an excessive standardization of their work, and away from that variety of syllabus content and teaching methods which is desirable if our educational system is to be in any real sense alive'. They recommend that the terms of reference of the Schools Council should include 'The objects of the Schools Council are to uphold and interpret the principle that each school should have the fullest possible measure, etc.

The Schools Council was to have a Governing Council of up to sixty-six members, a coordinating committee of ten, three curriculum committees corresponding to age groups of pupils, a GCE Committee and a CSE Committee, a General Purposes Committee, a Welsh

Committee, and subject committees (at first inherited en bloc from the SSEC). In each of the major committees representatives of teachers' associations were in a majority of one, and of two on the Governing Council. The Council should be free to select its own subjects for study, and should have full operational control of its own staff. Its staff were to be drawn from all sectors of the education service and to be on short-term appointments of three or four years, thus always being 'men and women with recent practical experience'; after the three or four years they would return to their former posts. The Report thanked the Minister for his offer to 'support, within a budget to be negotiated annually, research and development work commissioned by the Council', and added 'We think it desirable that the Council should also draw on other sources of support for such work'.

The Lockwood proposals were put to a reconvened meeting in June 1964 of the representative body that had set it up, which unanimously recommended their adoption. Quintin Hogg (the former, and later, Lord Hailsham), now Minister of Education, implemented them in full immediately, and the Council began on 1 October 1964, less than four months after the recommendations of the reconvened meeting, with Sir John Maud, a former Permanent Secretary of the Ministry of Education, as its first Chairman. It is fascinating to look back now from today's perspective and reflect that these very liberal and progressive ideas were put forward by a senior civil servant in the Ministry of Education, and implemented without delay by two successive Conservative Ministers of Education serving in a Conservative Government.

That is how the Schools Council was set up.

Examinations and Curriculum

The Council always carried out its foundation principle that schools should have the fullest possible responsibility for their own curriculum, which should be evolved by their own staff to meet the needs of their own pupils. This was no less true in the purely examinations field than in purely curriculum work.

The constitution mirrored this aim, and what was seen as the desirable position, in that committees dealing with examination work were (I) sub-ordinated to the curriculum committees; (II) composed in the main of the same sort of people, including one or two of the same people, serving in the different fields of the education service, with teachers serving in school in the majority (usually a majority of one), as were the curriculum committees. The constitution says that Curriculum

Steering Committee B (age-range 11–16) has five specific functions, two of which are 'it shall act as central coordinating authority for the administration of examinations normally taken by pupils on attaining the age of 16 ('first examinations'); and (it shall) make recommendations to the Governing Council on matters of examinations policy involving first examinations about which the Governing Council may wish to tender advice to the Secretary of State'. The First Examinations Committee is given two functions only — 'to undertake such work in connexion with the coordination and administration of first examinations as Curriculum Steering Committee B may direct and to make such decisions in these matters as may be delegated to it; and to make recommendations to Curriculum Steering Committee B on matters of examinations policy, and on any matters relating to the coordination and administration of first examinations on which Curriculum Steering Committee B has reserved powers of decision.' The wording, and the degree of emphasis, was changed, not in a major way, during the Council's life, but the principle remained the same, and remained laid down in the constitution. Note, too, that on any major policy matter in examinations, (which would constitute a recommendation, or advice, to the Secretary of State), the Curriculum Steering Committees could also only recommend to Governing Council, representing the Council as a whole and all its member interests, and only Governing Council could send a recommendation, or advice, to the Secretary of State.

More important, the Council's major work on examinations (in addition to a continuous stream of smaller-scale work on technical and administrative details of the examinations system and enquiries such as those into 'A' level grading, and comparability of 'A' level grades), were all in furtherance of examinations which would leave the schools free to choose their own curriculum, or at least increase such freedom as they already had in this. CSE was just being introduced when the Council started, and it threw itself into a mass of work on the foundations, the problems, the new perspectives and details of the practice of this nationally-validated examination in which the schools could choose to take an external syllabus externally examined, to submit their own syllabus to be externally examined, or to submit their own syllabus and then set and conduct their own examination on it. The magnificent series of Examination Bulletins dealt with all the problems thrown up, showed the new possibilities that were opened up, and did monumental spade work, in constructing the foundations of the new examination, and in showing teachers, whether concerned with the running of the examination in a region or whether purely in their own teaching in their own classrooms, how this could be operated and be successful. Successful it was, despite the hostile remarks of those who were out of sympathy with its aims, and it reached its present position of having as many entries as 'O' level, and of being universally recognized as equivalent to 'O' level (CSE grade 1 to 'O' level grades A to C), and throughout this of every teacher teaching for it being free to choose the curriculum he wanted — subject, of course, to proper checks on standards. It should be remembered that freedom to choose includes freedom to choose to have a completely external examination, if the teacher prefers this. Such examinations in the CSE were subject to far more teacher direction and influence (as the CSE boards by their constitutions all had serving teacher majorities) than had ever been the case before with a major school examination system — though GCE, expecially 'O' level, has now been much modified in this direction, under this influence.

Since the Council adopted the proposal for a single examining system at 16 in June 1970, it has virtually divided the necessary work towards this with the two sets of examinations boards. It did much of the early work on how this could be done — Examination Bulletin 23[8] published in October 1971 was a major landmark — and it divided the work of the massive programme of feasibility studies with the boards. The introduction of a single system, in a suitable form, would make possible a much better organization of teaching in the schools, especially in the comprehensive schools that house over 80 per cent of the pupils concerned. It would make it possible to get much nearer to choosing for each pupil a curriculum, and a teaching group, suitable to his/her needs than the dual system, and would make possible economies in staffing at the same time.

The Sixth Form

At 18 the man bulk of the Council's work, which was very considerable, was a series of heroic endeavours, some on a massive scale, to bring about change in the curriculum of the sixth form. The relation between examinations and curriculum in the sixth form is different from that at 16+. At 16+, once the group requirements that were an essential feature of the structure of School Certificate and 'matriculation' had been removed, as the SSEC recommended in 1947 and as was implemented in 1950 when the GCE was introduced, the shape and structure of the individual pupil's curriculum was freed, and could be devised with a view to meeting his/her individual needs. The single subjects of 'O' level (and since, of the CSE) are so many building bricks with which any number of different structures may be constructed. There is no single 'user' of the examination, or corporate group of users, which dominates the field. This is not the case with 'A' levels, where the universities so completely dominate the field that in effect they can, and do, dictate what shall be done, and so impose a structure of their own choosing on the whole examination and so on the whole of the sixth form curriculum.

The English sixth form curriculum is unique in the world as far more specialized than in any other country, coming down from the typical six, seven or eight subjects at 16+ to its three 'A' levels typically in 'related' subjects. This is maintained in being by the universities, partly in their official requirements and partly by their practice in making their selections from competitive fields for entry. A growing movement to replace this by a less specialized curriculum for 16–18 for applicants for degree courses starting in the 1960s, was joined by another to provide something more suitable than 'A' level for the 'new sixth-formers', pupils who would previously have left school at 16, but now wished to stay after 16, but for whom 'A' levels were obviously not an appropriate diet. These ideas were expressed in the Crowther Report[9] in 1959 and in the SSEC's Third Report[10] in 1960, both of which ended up recommending the continuance of A levels (the last major reports to do so), but wished to meet these two objectives somehow.

The Schools Council, at its first meeting in 1964, declared sixth form curriculum and examinations a first priority. In 1966 Working Paper 5 recommended a pattern of 'majors', 'minors' and general studies 'as a basis for discussion'. (Proposals for sixth form subjects at either of two different levels are never called 'principal' and 'subsidiary', the names they had in the pre-1950 Higher School Certificate; new names are always invented for them). Not much discussion took place, in my opinion because the Council had not prepared the ground or launched its proposals adequately; it still thought that if proposals were published, that was sufficient.

For its next attempt, it entered into formal discussions with representatives of the universities, in the shape of representatives appointed by the Standing Conference on University Entrance, usually known as 'SCUE'. This produced Working Paper 16[12] in 1967, in two sections, one from the Council, making proposals, and one from the representatives of SCUE, pointing out some of their consequences. The proposals were for two 'majors', plus 'electives' — 'minors' which could be either one-year or two-year courses, the latter taking half the time of a 'major', and examined on a CSE Mode 3 basis. 'Electives' were the special pet of John Dancy, then Master of Marlborough. This meant trusting the school with the degree course candidate's general education, and confining his specialisms to two main subjects to make room for it. The universities were devoid of enthusiasm for either of these changes, which killed the proposals.

The next two sets of proposals were on a different and much larger scale, including surveys of alternative systems, where these existed and worked well, and detailed answers to all the questions that a new basis for sixth form curriculum and examinations would raise, based in many cases on very detailed and thorough field surveys and 'dummy runs'. The proposals affecting applicants for degree courses were produced by a Joint Working Party with equal numbers of representatives of the schools' side — teachers in maintained and independent schools, and a Chief Education Officer from the LEAs — and of the universities, appointed by SCUE, with a university chairman Professor Butler, Head of Physics at Imperial College, London, later Sir Clifford Butler, Vice-Chancellor of Loughborough University). Both sets of proposals were based on five subjects, at either of two levels. The first, commonly known as 'Q and F',[13] was a stepped system, in which five subjects were all taken in an examination at the end of the first year in the sixth at an equal level, and then the pupil continued with two or three of them to a higher level to be examined at the end of the second year in the sixth. This fell foul chiefly of the teaching profession, especially the National Union of Teachers, and of the universities, both of which bodies objected to a system which gave an 18-year-old school leaver a major examination at the end of each of his last three years in school. The second, ('N and F', or 'the Butler/Briault proposals', enshrined in the 'Butler' and the two 'Briault' reports),[14] had five subjects all taken after two years in the sixth, two at the higher level and three at the lower level. The higher level would need three-quarters of the 'study time' of the present 'A' level, and the lower level a half. The second 'Briault' report gave detailed recommendations for the Certificate of Extended Education — curriculum, structure and examination.

These two sets of proposals went into every detail about the examinations required — the technicalities of their grading, their overlap, the various uses that could be made of them, and many others — but they were curricular enquiries and curricular recommendations, whose aim was the broadening of the sixth form curriculum. New examinations were recommended only as a means to this, a necessary means for the reasons stated. This was shown very strongly in the syllabus enquiries carried out as part of 'N and F', in which over 300 subject experts in fifty-six different groups produced several different possible syllabuses for each of the sixteen main subjects at each level, so that people could see what these would be like. Other surveys showed what the timetables of schools of different sizes and natures would be like, what choices of subjects sixth formers were likely to make, and a number of other aspects of the proposals.[15] A national debate was stimulated and conducted by the Council. Copies of the proposals and of the surveys were sent to every school, every university and Further Education college and every interested body in the country. Schools Council staff and members addressed over 400 meetings about the proposals. A broadsheet was produced in March 1979[16] itemizing the questions that were being asked, under fourteen different heads, including several alternatives to the recommendations, and inviting detailed replies. Over 600 were received.

I do not think it could possibly be denied that the Schools Council did everything that could be done to bring about changes in the sixth form curriculum and examinations that would broaden the present degree of specialization and also make possible alternative courses and examinations more appropriate to many of those now in the sixth forms. It never once lost sight of the idea that the aim was a wholly curricular aim; new examinations, and changes in examinations, were recommended in detail only as the necessary means to bring about change in the curriculum. They would also have made it much easier for, and given more scope to, those schools that wished to shape the different curricula of the various sixth formers more nearly in accordance with their individual needs.

It has been adduced as a criticism of the Council that none of these succeeded in being adopted. This is not wholly true; the CEE has been with us, with a good field of candidates, for over a decade, and many of the individual recommendations in detail for improvement of the main-level subject examinations have been adopted at 'A' level by a number of the GCE boards. It remains true that the recommended major changes have not been made. The Schools Council had no powers to make any change, it was non-prescriptive. It could survey the scene, consider the possibilities and make enquiries into them, make recommendations and seek to persuade people to adopt them. In this sphere it did all that could be done in each of these, but did not succeed in the last. Is it still to be taxed with this as a 'failure', in that it 'failed' to carry conviction?

I would mention four reasons why this was so. The first is that although the university representatives, nominated by SCUE, joined in making the recommendations (have they also 'failed'?), the universities as a whole, especially those in them who teach 'linear' subjects, in which each year's work uses as a necessary basis what has been done in the previous years, have been totally opposed to any change that would reduce the syllabus content of their subjects covered in the sixth form, regardless of any other consideration. Many of the professional bodies consulted took a similar view, for similar reasons. Secondly, many teachers in the schools always prefer to stay with whatever is established at their time, from natural conservatism. Thirdly, a number of people did not share the basic aims; they genuinely preferred a sixth form curriculum as specialized as ours is now to something broader. I think such people are now in a minority, though probably a large one. Fourthly, no Secretary of State did anything to assist these proposals, and one virtually closed the discussion for some time to come. They did this partly from not wishing to start up anything that might cause themselves a lot of trouble, and partly from the terrible fear aroused by the universities, who said that if the syllabus content of 'A' levels were to be reduced in this way, then either the syllabus content (they of course didn't call it that, they called it the 'standard') of the first degree must be officially lowered, or the typical three-year first degree course must become a four-year course. No Secretary of State could view without dread the prospect either of admitting that he had 'lowered standards', or of the resource implications of four-year degree courses. Both of these assertions of course were and are disputed. The case has been stated, by university teachers amongst others, that to reduce the syllabus content of 'A' level to three-quarters of what it is now would necessitate neither a lowering of the standard of the first degree nor any lengthening of the present first degree courses. An analysis of the replies to the Council about the 'N and F' proposals shows that a majority of the respondents was against these proposals, and also that a majority was against 'A' levels continuing as they were. What was also made clear was that with any alternative to 'A' levels that had yet been proposed, a majority of the respondents was against it.

Whilst the Council was still collating these replies into a document for publication (by which time their general trend was well known), Mark Carlisle in June 1979, six weeks after taking office, wrote to the Council and said that he thought 'it would be wrong to replace 'A' levels with examinations based on the 'N and F' proposals or any similar new system within the foreseeable future', and that he thought the arguments put forward against 'N and F' were very strong, especially those relating to 'the preservation of the standards of traditional sixth form courses', and 'the possible effect on the length of the first degree course'. These were the only arguments or points that he referred to. (This was actually a bipartisan decision, since Shirley Williams had announced the same decision orally to the Secondary Heads Association Conference in March 1979[17], characteristically adding that she favoured a new examination for 18+ in three major subjects and two minor ones, but that there was not enough agreement on any new examination for there to be any question of abolishing 'A' levels). Mark Carlisle's announcement of his decision built a stone wall across the road to any major reform of the sixth form curriculum in the direction of broadening it, and brought to a halt the movements of the previous fifteen to twenty years, at least for some time. 'The foreseeable future' will not be less than five years, but may not be much more than ten.

'Presiding Over the Obsequies'

After the publication of the Trenaman Report[18] in October 1981, recommending 'that the Council continue with its present functions, and . . . should not be made the subject of further external review for at least five years', six months' silence followed. On 22 April 1982 Sir Keith Joseph announced in the House of Commons his intention of 'disbanding the Schools Council, and replacing it with two bodies, one for examinations, the other for curriculum development'. A striking feature of the announcement was that it gave no reasons for the decision. As far as I am aware, none has ever been given since then. In a written Parliamentary answer in August 1982 Sir Keith Joseph said the two functions were 'very different' and should be managed by people with different qualifications and backgrounds. The earnest seeker after truth can examine the final membership of the two new bodies to see how clearly this distinction stands out. Sir Keith also said that 'experience since 1964 has cast doubt on the wisdom' of having curriculum and examinations dealt with by one body. Both of these remarks seem to be examples of asserting, rather than arguing, his case. The general reaction to the announcement was one of astonishment and incredulity.

After the announcement of the decision, two things happened that could well seem odd. The first was indeed in the announcement, but the implementation gradually made it much clearer — the Schools Council had not been abolished, in the sense of having been done away with, and nothing taking its place. Mr (now Sir) Philip Holland, MP, the foe of quangos, lost no time in pointing out, when the announcement was made, that it replaced one quango by two, even if it was two for the price of one. When the two memberships were finally announced, they were not a totally different kind of group from the average Schools Council committee. The NUT were absent, by their own decision; one member of the Curriculum Committee, counting the number of chairmen of education committees present, said 'we have exchanged the teacher politicians for the real politicians of education'. A number of School Council members, including some very prominent ones, appeared on the new bodies, including at least some who were unlikely to follow a DES line.

The total budget for the two committees, for their first year, though less than that for the Schools Council, was in the same range. A considerable number of Schools Council staff were appointed to corresponding positions on the two new bodies — as Sir Keith had said, in his announcement, that he hoped would happen. The Chief Officer appointed to the Curriculum Committee, Sir Wilfred Cockcroft's Deputy appointed to the Examinations Committee (Sir Wilfred being Chairman and Chief Officer), and the officer at the Head of Finance and Administration for both bodies were in each case the person who was doing this job in the Schools Council.

The DES had indicated clearly soon after the announcement that it intended the Secondary Science Curriculum Review and the Industry Project, the two biggest Schools Council projects currently running, to continue as they were, and this list was gradually extended, partly by the DES' fiat, and then by the bodies' own decisions, when they started work, to include a good number of other Schools Council current projects.

After reading the list of these, one (especially one hostile to the Schools Council) might well ask 'What's different?' The answer is that there are quite specific major differences in the way the work is done, which can affect what work is done:

(i)   separation of examinations and curriculum in two separate bodies (served by a common secretariat), with examinations very much before curriculum in a number of ways;

(ii)   neither body is representative, in the sense of interests being given membership and asked to name their representative(s) both are hand-picked by the Minister and are his personal appointments. Only the LEAs, finding half the cost of the curriculum body, refused this and insisted on choosing their own representatives on it;

(iii)   it is provided explicitly in the constitution of each of the two new bodies that the Secretary of State can at any time dissolve them by his own sole decision;

(iv)   the total funding has been reduced, and it is explicitly stated in the original announcement that the function of the curriculum body should be 'the limited task of identifying gaps, helping to fill them and assisting with the dissemination of curriculum innovation'.

Walter Ulrich (DES Deputy Secretary) had recommended a fair amount of this as the DES recommendations to Mrs Trenaman, for changes in the Schools Council. It is recorded that 'Mrs Trenaman considered that the scheme proposed by the Department amounted to a closure of the present Council and the creation of a new and different body'. It is in fact a purely semantic question — or if it is anything more, it is a purely subjective question — whether you say the Schools Council has been transformed, so as to continue, but with a number of quite major changes, or that the Schools Council has been abolished; two new bodies have been set up, which will do some of the work the Council did, and which have several other factors in common with the Council.

That genial cynic, Dr Rhodes Boyson, said at one stage to a protesting delegation 'There had to be a ritual slaughter'. It is profitable to consider carefully the significance of each word in this remark, which is not true of all the good Doctor's sayings. It would have been possible to have said 'we are going to insist on the Schools Council's adopting three or four major changes', in the way in which the DES recommendations were put to Mrs Trenaman by Mr Ulrich. Why was this not done? Possibly because of all the hassle that would have been involved in the legal and financial tangles, some of which did emerge in the closure of the Council — though the DES did not appear to have anticipated this. Not necessarily because they could never have carried it through as changes in the Council, since under the 1978 constitution DES and LEAs had between them two-thirds of the votes in the Finance and Priorities Committee, the Committee which controlled the Council. They would have needed the support of both sets of LEAs, but they finally obtained that anyway for what they have done — the Association of Metropolitan Authorities (AMA) objected at first, but then appear to have followed the maxim 'if you can't beat 'em, join 'em'. Much more probably, because the politicians concerned wished to be able to tell Tory right-wing back-benchers that they had abolished the Council. Hence the Doctor's accurate remark. Doing it this way, and not by changing the constitution of the Council, cost nearly £3 million in public money which would otherwise not have been necessary (for example, in redundancy payments, and in the delay in moving to new premises). Whether those who took the decision thought the difference in the two possible ways of bringing it about well worth that price, or whether that was something else that had not been anticipated, is left to speculation.

The other thing after the announcement of the decision that might seem rather odd is that it took two years to implement it. Why?

This is clearly to be added to the list of things the DES had not anticipated, since Dr Boyson told Dr Peter Andrews, then Acting Chairman of the Schools Council, attending at the DES at Dr Boyson's invitation to discuss the proposals announced in the decision, that the Examinations Council was the first objective and the priority for ministers, and that it would probably be set up in the autumn (ie, of 1982), and the Curriculum Council (still a Council, not yet demoted to a Committee) by the end of the year (ie December 1982); but that there was some doubt about the timing of the curriculum body. In the event the Examinations Council held its first meeting in April 1983, the curriculum body held its first business meeting in February 1984, and the Schools Council was closed down on 31 March 1984 — three weeks short of two years since Sir Keith Joseph had made his announcement. Why? I do not know the answer. I would love to. I know several possible answers each of which some people find adequate, but I find it difficult to do so. Several people whom I asked said immediately that this was simply the DES' normal level of competence and efficiency, and particularly of speed, in administration. I smiled dutifully at this expected witticism, and then said 'But what do you think actually is the reason?' — to be told that the speaker was being serious, and that unexpected and unexplained delays of this order and scale were par for the course with the DES. I find it hard to accept this as the sole reason for the passage of two years. Clearly there was a good deal of cross-firing behind the scenes, for example with the AMA, before they finally fell into line with the proposals — apart from their successful insistence, along with the Association of County Councils (ACC), of choosing their own representatives to the Curriculum Committee. Two puzzles may well solve each other here, since some would regard the AMA's falling into line as another puzzle in itself, the answer to which may be well known to those party to the AMA's internal discussions. I do not know. The AMA is reported to have objected at first to the choice of Chairman for the Curriculum Committee; Sir Keith after receiving the NUT's refusal to take any part in either body, repeated his invitation to them and offered discussions. All this would take time. Add to that that the DES were moving in unfamiliar waters (unfamiliar to them at any rate), and possibly had little idea at first of how to proceed, and no great anticipation of how the steps taken for the implementation would develop, (for example the legal and financial complications, and those connected with contractual obligations, in closing down the Council), as is suggested by the length of time it took them to reach the various decisions that became necessary as the process went on. It may well also be the case that those who took the decision would not have minded much if the curriculum body had never come into existence, so that they might not have pressed impatiently for faster progress on this front. But two years! The British left India in less time than that!

The Process of Closure

What happened in the Council in the two years? The announcement was received in the Council with some of the astonishment and incredulity as in the educational world outside. Some people manifested symptoms of shock for a time. There was a short period of waiting to see if the decision was going to stand, or might be reversed or modified. Papers were drawn up setting out the case against, and alternatives; representations were made, and deputations received at the DES. It gradually became clear that the decision would not be reversed or modified, and so the Council turned to seeking to find out how, and particularly when, it was to be implemented, so that it could arrange its remaining affairs accordingly.

To find this out proved an almost impossible task. For eighteen months the Council was continually awaiting, and pressing for, announcements of various essential decisions, in particular of the time scale involved. This came at the end of November 1983. During this period the Council was expecting to hear any month, any week, any day the length of life it had left. In this situation the Council set itself three main tasks — to reduce the scale of its activities gradually in a way which would cause the minimum damage to them, to ensure that all work that was in hand but not completed was carried through to completion and to protect the interest of its staff, as far as it had the power to.

The DES quickly sent an instruction that no new work was to be undertaken without their express permission (a direct veto which they had never attempted to impose before, but whose content made sense in the situation anyway).

As the Council could not initiate any new work, committees concerned primarily with this function were virtually at a standstill, with no work to do and nothing to call them together for. Meetings of subject committees had been suspended *pro tem* after the Trenaman Report (which recommended their abolition). Committees concerned with the writing up and publication of reports soon found they had more work to do than usual. The DES soon decided that the two big projects, the Industry Project and the Secondary Science Curriculum Review, should continue after the Council had closed. Towards the end of the long period of uncertainty this decision was gradually reached on a number of other projects which obviously could not possibly be completed by March 1984, and finally the new curriculum body reached the same decision with a further number of projects — in February 1984! The Council bent its energies to seeing that, if possible, all other projects in hand should be completed by the Council, and that their reports should be fully written up and, where appropriate, published, so that the fruits of the work done should not be lost. This meant stepping up the pace, and streams of continuing activity were thus dealt with by a steadily decreasing staff, and some of the senior staff were seeing through this accelerated output, dealing with the problems of closing the Council, and also with some of the initial problems of the new bodies, all at once. A similar situation applied, to a lesser extent, to some of the members. So little of this was realized by people outside the Council that towards the end of 1983 one of the more reputable educational journals, which should have known better, included a sentence referring to 'the former Schools Council' as a body that no longer existed! This was eclipsed by Sir Keith Joseph, who officially opened a week-long conference in London five days before the Council was due to close by his decision, a conference which was part of a Schools Council project on 'Mother Tongue Teaching', (teaching immigrant children in the schools in their own language). The project was largely financed by the EEC, and the conference was attended by leading educationists from all the EEC countries. I was waiting, fascinated, to see how he would handle this delicate situation — would he be generous, and give fair praise where it was due, or churlish, or what? In the event he made a twenty-minute speech in which he not only never mentioned the Council, but never mentioned the project whose week-long conference he was officially opening.

Between Sir Keith's announcement in April 1982 and the Council's closure in March 1984 it issued over eighty major publications, including such as Vera Southgate's *Extending Beginning Reading*,[19] which won the UK Reading Association's Research Award and became an educational best-seller, and the book *Primary Practice*,[20] produced within the Council as a follow-up to *The Practical Curriculum*, and distributed to every school in the country. It continued with a great array of projects, large and small, carrying most of them to completion. It continued its functions of technical monitoring of the work of the GCE and CSE boards, including detailed scrutiny of 'A' level examinations subject by subject, maintained its information centres and services and kept on field officers 'out in the country' until 31 January 1984.

The Staff of the Council were left for a long time in an unenviable position, hard though the Council strove to avoid or mitigate this. They did not know when their work with the Council would cease, or whether they would be taken on by the new bodies. Their redundancy situation, and redundancy terms, were the subject of dispute for a long time, with at one time three separate sets of lawyers disputing them — the Council's lawyers, the DES' lawyers, and the Treasury's lawyers.

Few had realized that no-one could close the Council except the Council itself. It might commit suicide, but it could not be killed by another hand. Neither the DES, nor Sir Keith, nor all Mrs Thatcher's horses and men, could abolish the Council; its constitution prevented this. This lesson has been carefully noted, and power for the Secretary of State to do exactly this has been carefully provided in the constitution of both the new bodies. In the case of the Council, no-one had ever envisaged anyone's wishing to abolish it, which is why no such provision had been made.

What the Secretary of State could do was to cut off his funds to the Council. These were a little under half its income, since the two LEA bodies between them paid a matching sum, and the Council had an income, small in comparison to these sums, from some of its activities, chiefly from its publications. The LEA associations are not compelled to follow the DES in this, either in paying or in deciding not to pay; they still have that much freedom in deciding what to do with their own funds. In terms of political reality the ACC could hardly be expected to do any other, unpalatable though this would be for some of their representatives. But why did the AMA, after criticizing the decision, fall into line and stump up for the new curriculum body? And show no interest in any possibility of keeping on a reduced Council? We may know the answer one day. One obvious guess is that they decided that as they could not reverse the decision, and there would be two new bodies, and the ACC would be part-paymaster of the curriculum body, they had better get in on the act and this precluded having a foot in each of two camps, and particularly paying money to both of them. The AMA's goodwill to the Council was never in any doubt.

If neither of the big LEA associations was prepared to give financial support to a continuing Council, any such continuing Council could only be on a financial scale that would be a minute percentage of the Council as it existed. There were a few possibilities, that could be explored, of relatively very small financial subvention, and a few more of some assistance in kind — use of premises, seconding staff on salary to the Council — and a number of people would have given their services as staff, part-time or full-time, voluntarily for no pay, because they believed in the Council and what it stood for and wished to see it continue.

But a Council without the DES, the AMA and the ACC, without its 'special relationship' with the examination boards, (which was formally given to it, as it had been to the SSEC, by the DES), and on a tiny scale of funding and therefore of operation, would be a continuation of the Council in constitutional technicality, but not in any real practical sense. Not all the other member interests might have wished to remain in such circumstances, and it could have become difficult to avoid becoming virtually an organization of teachers' associations, and possibly not the full range of them. Such a body could do some useful work, but it could not have been claimed that it was in any real sense the Schools Council continuing. Since it would have been so in law, it would be subject to all the legal complications and hassle that had to be dealt with in closing it. So all in all it seemed that it might be that no very great purpose would be served by seeking to continue the Council in this way. If such a body as it was reasonable to think it might become could indeed function and serve a useful purpose, it might perhaps be better to set it up as a fresh body altogether, without seeking to maintain any kind of constitutional link.

This tentative conclusion was completely reinforced, and any alternative put out of court, by the issue of redundancy pay. The decision not to attempt to force through the desired changes as changes in the Schools Council, but to close it, and set up two new bodies, meant liability to redundancy pay for the Schools Council staff. The terms of this were argued over interminably, as has already been referred to, and gradually the various issues were resolved, some very late in the day. The total redundancy bill was calculated at £2¼ million; the Schools Council's pension fund stood at £900,000. The DES said it would pay the difference. If the Council had continued, in whatever form or scale, but legally the Schools Council continuing, it would have had this liability for every employee it was not able to retain in its employment — which would have been most of them. A hopeful suggestion was made that the DES should be asked if in these circumstances it would still pay the difference, but this seemed so unrealistic that there was no point in even raising the issue. Advice was given that this meant that any continuing Council that could be envisaged would be bankrupt, with no prospect of ever getting out of this condition. This finally settled any question of seeking to keep the Council in being in any way.

Having once reached this conclusion, there was no purpose to be served by doing other than cooperate with the DES in closing down the Council and getting the two new bodies set up, and some purpose in doing so, and in helping the nascent new bodies to achieve their not wholly straightforward birth.

The DES finally, nineteen months after the announcement of the decision, proposed a date for the closure of the Council and the issuing of redundancy notices to the remaining staff, and 'formally requested' the Council to 'initiate the necessary action'. (In April 1982 the Council had 122 staff (full-time equivalent); on 1 December 1983 eighty-seven; on 1 January 1984 there were sixty-odd; at the end of February seventeen were still in post, and they left the service of the Council on 31 March). The constitution had to be altered formally to make it possible even for the Council to dissolve itself; there were time limits that had to be observed in doing this. This was duly arranged and done, and then the ritual self-slaughter could take place, which it did in meetings of the three major committees of the Council in succession on the same day, which by resolutions carried nem con (not unanimously, as one teacher representative said it went too much against the grain to vote for the closure of the Council, and he therefore did not vote) dissolved the Council with effect from 31 March and placed its remaining assets in the hands of liquidators and of the Council's Trustees. I was reminded strongly of those Roman emperors who would send notes to certain individuals, saying that the Emperor expected to receive the news of their suicide within the next few days — though even those emperors did not send their personal representative to attend the event and make sure that everything went well (from the emperor's point of view) and reached the end he desired.

The Future of the Council

The story of the ritual slaughter of the Council would not be complete without some reference to its continuing life and vitality since then, its many appearances and its looked-for resurrection after not too great an interval of time.

Nor do I mean only that it lives in the memory of man; it does indeed, but this is not all. It does indeed live in the changed attitude of hundreds of thousands of teachers all over this country and in many others to their work in the school and in the class-room, due to the work of the Council. It lives in the minds of educationists the world over as an example of a publicly-funded independent representative self-governing body which never had, or wished for, any power to tell anyone to do anything, but could only put ideas forward, and recommendations; it could achieve influence and impact only by the quality of its work commending itself to the practitioners — which it did with resounding success, in sales of its materials and their use in the class-room, in scores of fields time and time again.

But these materials and these ideas are in use in the class-room now, in the present, and will be next year and the year after. The structures and methods the Council worked out are now being used in external examinations in schools. A steady stream of Schools Council publications has issued from the press since April 1984, and will continue until August 1985, with the help of the educational publishers, and in some cases of the new curriculum body. Its Industry Project, its Secondary Science Curriculum Review, its guidelines for schools' internal reviews, Geography 16–19, Mother Tongue Teaching and quite a number of other projects are being continued by the new curriculum body. The London and the regional information centres, the Cardiff office, the Publications Company are all continuing. Some of the members of the two new bodies hope to see them continue many of the Council's ideas, as well as its kind of work, after these inherited projects have all been completed.

Two attempts, to my knowledge, are being made at the time of writing to set up small-scale independent bodies that will do some of the work and carry out some of the functions that the Council did. Whether either will succeed and see such a body set up, still less whether it will establish itself and function successfully over a period of time, is at the time of writing an open question.

Lastly the case has already been publicly stated and the campaign launched for the restoration of the Council. This would only need a Secretary of State whose views on this followed the great majority — over 80 per cent — of those who replied to Mrs Trenaman, instead of the small minority, as Sir Keith's decision did. This would not be in the least difficult; it would only need the announcement of a decision to reverse Sir Keith's decision. This would mean merging the two new bodies into one, so that the same body dealt with curriculum and examinations, in a way that put curriculum first and made the examinations follow it, and altering its basis of membership from the present hand-picked one appointed by the Secretary of State to a representative one, appointed one by one by the member interests named — as the LEAs now do on the curriculum body. This would need a new constitution, which it would not be difficult, or a long task, to draw up. There are various people, to any of whom this task could be given; a new Lockwood Committee would probably be the best. Three months should be more than enough for them, as a lot of water has flowed under the bridge since Lockwood. Whether the resulting body was called a Schools Council, or something totally different, and whether its constitution was anything like the Schools Council's, or Mrs Trenaman's recommendations, is not particularly important. What is important is to have a genuinely and demonstrably independent curriculum and examinations body, with curriculum coming first, financed on an adequate scale, and it should be on a representative basis, self-governing, and non-prescriptive. It may not be too many years before we see it.

References

1 WRIGLEY , J. (1983) 'Confessions of a curriculum man', *Curriculum*, Vol. 4, No. 2, and in this volume.
2 (1960) *Secondary School Examinations other than the GCE*, London, HMSO.
3 (1962) *The Certificate of Secondary Education: Notes for the Guidance of Regional Examining Bodies* (Fifth Report of the SSEC), London, HMSO.
4 (1938) *Secondary Education, with special reference to grammar schools and technical high schools*, London, HMSO.
5 (1943) *Curriculum and Examinations in Secondary Schools*, London, HMSO.
6 Ministry of Education (1964) *Report of the Working Party on the Schools' Curricula and Examinations* (The Lockwood Committee), London, HMSO.
7 WRIGLEY, J. (1983) *op. cit.*
8 (1971) *A Common System of Examining at 16+*, Schools Council Examinations Bulletin 23, Evans/Methuen Educational.
9 (1959) *15 to 18: a report of the Central Advisory Council for Education* (England), London, HMSO.
10 (1960) *The General Certificate of Education and Sixth Form Studies*, Third Report of the SSEC, London, HMSO.
11 (1966) *Sixth-Form Curriculum and Examinations*, Schools Council Working Paper No. 5, London, HMSO.
12 (1967) *Some Further Proposals for Sixth-Form Work*, Schools Council Working Paper No.16, London, HMSO.
13 (1969) *Proposals for Curriculum and Examinations in the Sixth Form*, a joint statement by the two working parties from the Standing Conference on University Entrance and the Schools Council: Schools Council.
14 (1972) *16–19: Growth and Response: 1 Curricular Bases*, Schools Council Working Paper 45, London, Evans/Methuen Educational; (1973) *16–19: Growth and Response: 2 Examination Structure*, Schools Council Working Paper No. 46, London, Evans/Methuen Educational; (1973) *Preparation for Degree Courses*, Schools Council Working Paper No. 47, Standing Conference on University Entrance Sixth Form 73/2, London, Evans/Methuen Educational.

15 (1978) *Examinations at 18+: resource implications of an N and F curriculum and examination structure*, Schools Council Examinations Bulletin 38, Evans/Methuen Educational, January; (1978) *Examinations at 18+: N and F studies*, School Council Working Paper No. 60, Evans/Methuen Educational, April.
16 (1979) *Examinations at 18+: the N and F Debate: a progress report*, Schools Council, March.
17 WILLIAMS, S. reported in the *Daily Telegraph*, 27 March 1979.
18 (1981) *Review of the Schools Council*, a report from Mrs Nancy Trenaman to the Secretaries of State for Education and for Wales and to the LEA associations, DES, October.
19 SOUTHGATE, V., ARNOLD, H. and JOHNSON, S. (1982) *Extending Beginning Reading*, London, Heinemann.
20 (1983) *Primary Practice: a Sequel to 'the Practical Curriculum'*, Schools Council Working Paper No. 75, London, Methuen Educational.

Confessions of a Curriculum Man

Jack Wrigley

The Curriculum Study Group formed around 1962 was the forerunner of the Schools Council and consisted of a number of Ministry administrators, HMI and one outsider as a research adviser. That outsider was myself. The men in charge of the Curriculum Study Group were Derek Morrell, an administrator, and Robert Morris, a Staff Inspector. These two gentlemen later became the Joint Secretaries to the Schools Council. The Curriculum Study Group planned all the early curriculum projects in collaboration with the Nuffield Foundation and laid the foundations for very many of the early large curriculum innovations in this country. In parallel to this work the Curriculum Study Group planned the Certificate of Secondary Education and my main work was connected with this new examination. In my view, from the inside, the Curriculum Study Group was a harmless, potentially valuable organization. Nevertheless, it met with intense opposition from an alliance of teachers led by Sir Ronald Gould of the NUT, and local education authorities led by Sir William Alexander. The fear was central control of the curriculum. One headmaster, wrote 'Have we fought two World Wars for this?'. The opposition was so intense that within a very short time the Curriculum Study Group had to transform itself into a more democratic teacher controlled organization, the Schools Council. It is interesting to compare and contrast the attitude of teachers and local education authorities to the Curriculum Study Group in the 1960s and to the Assessment of Performance Unit (APU) in the 1980s. The APU is working on the monitoring of important curriculum aspects of this country's education and the dangers of central control must be as prevalent today as they were in the 1960s, yet the opposition has been comparatively muted. In an article in *The Times Educational Supplement* I finished with the sentence 'does the CSG equal APU' and a letter from Professor Philip Taylor of the University of Birmingham commented that in the 1960s we were in the age of the teacher whereas in the late 1970s and the 1980s we are in the age of the inspector. I hold to the view that I had in the 1960s that there is in this country little danger of central control of the curiculum by the administrators in the Department of Education and Science. The teachers are simply too powerful for this danger to be particularly real and most of the comments and guidance with regard to curriculum development will have a much less powerful effect than the teaching conducted by those actually in the classrooms.

What the Curriculum Study Group did have, though, was a sense of purpose, a lack of bureaucratic control, an easy access to the Ministers of Education and an excitement which is difficult to convey but easy to remember. The work with regard to the Certificate of Secondary Education proceeded at a tremendously fast pace and is in very great contrast to the slow progress, if progress is the right word, we have made in the past ten or fifteen years in any further attempt to reform the examinations system. To be in the Curriculum Study Group was an exhilarating experience. In a sense I see no reason to confess my presence there. All the same many people would hold it against me if they ever remembered my presence in that organization, so perhaps it can count as a confession.

Four years later, and with some hesitation, I joined the Schools Council as Director of Studies, combining the post with a Chair at the University of Reading entitled Professor of Curriculum Research and Development. The early Schools Council had many of the attributes of the Curriculum Study Group. It had the same Joint Secretaries, the same desire to innovate, a determination to consider curriculum and examination matters together on the principle that assessment should follow the curriculum and be subservient to it, hence the Schools Council for curriculum *and* examinations. The Schools Council differed from the Curriculum Study Group in its bureaucratic structure, the large number of committees, and by virtue of the fact that teachers were in control of all of its main activities. I claim to have recognized some of the defects of that committee structure at a very early date. Indeed, discussing the question as to whether I should join the Council with Robert Morris I said to him 'but how on earth can one work with all those committees'. Robert Morris's reply was 'it is the price you pay for playing around with a £1 million a year'. This was 1967 and a £1 million then was a considerable amount of money, as it still is, but inflation has made inroads into such amounts.

In a sense the Council was created largely by the genius of a civil servant, Derek Morrell. While in the Curriculum Study Group I saw

Morrell day after day in the corridors of power, with his door open, writing the main constitution and draft for the Council itself. His ideas, of course, were embodied in the Lockwood Committee and in the decisions of Ministers, but the Council was his creation. Believe no-one who tells you the Council was a Tory plot or a Marxist conspiracy. This is simply not so. It stems from the imagination of a remarkable civil servant. His aim was to plan for a national initiative in curriculum innovation without incurring the risk of central control of the curriculum by his fellow administrators. Hence the establishment of a network of committees all with serving teacher majorities. Hence the decision to have most of the development carried out throughout the country on a commission basis. In an attempt to avoid a hardening of the arteries evident in so many institutions as they grow older it was decided that most of the senior staff should hold only temporary appointments. It was a truly unique institution and its modus operandi has been the envy of many a foreign visitor. The Council achieved some imaginative curriculum innovation without the danger of central control. It produced an impressive list of publications, achieved by excellent and friendly cooperation with the national publishing firms, and to some extent it cut through the tangled web of conflicting educational theory in an attempt to influence and change events in the classroom. It showed a fine independence of its paymasters, the DES and the LEAs; in those days the finances of the Council came equally 50 per cent from DES and 50 per cent from the LEAs, but on the main Programme Committee the active decisions were made by teachers. LEA and DES personnel played a remarkably small role in making those decisions.

The atmosphere in those early days was to some extent one of careless rapture. The curriculum development workers were confident. They proceeded to produce materials for children and for teachers without worrying too much about the nature of educational theory, the nature of individual differences, or the need for careful cool research.

One of the most remarkable characteristics of the early Schools Council was the liberal nature of its administration due in the main to the personality of the main creator of the Council, Derek Morrell, though he of course was helped in the planning stages by the Joint Secretary, HMI Robert Morris, who was equally liberal. Perhaps, though, the most important factor in this aspect of Council philosophy and practice was Ann George, the Administrative Officer, and Geoffrey Caston, the Joint Secretary (who succeeded Morrell). Between them they set up an organization which was designed to enable an *innovatory* institution to be *innovatory*. The administration was truly enabling in the best tradition of really great administration. The staff helped clarify the intention of the Committees and research workers, and then did their best to put the proposals into action as quickly and as efficiently as possible. The Council worked on the basis of a liberal philosophy and trust and honesty and integrity of the individual. The device of having two, later three Joint Secretaries, and the Director of Studies as the four senior posts without any implied hierarchy was a remarkable experiment chosen deliberately by Derek Morrell. I had a conversation with Morrell at a point when the system was first challenged after he had left the Council and at the time of the chairmanship of Alan Bullock. Morrell agreed that his idea was unusual but was convinced of its correctness in the circumstances of the Council. The ultimate authority for policy was the Programme Committee, and it could arbitrate between the Joint Secretaries if necessary. Morrell's main point was that each Joint Secretary would do more creative work as an equal rather than under the authority of a permanent director. Furthermore, the Council did not wish to put one man in charge for a long time since the innovatory fervour might decrease. Much of Morrell's thinking was inspired by this attempt to create an initiative which would remain young and fresh. Since the top appointments were not to be permanent, secondment was the order of the day. This policy resulted in my working with eleven Joint Secretaries in eight years. Before the system was finally changed in 1978 there had been in all thirteen Joint Secretaries and three Directors of Studies. A similar high rate of change of Curriculum and Field officers also took place.

One other aspect of this policy was that the holders of the top posts would eventually take up important jobs back in their universities, their local education authorities, the schools, and the Department of Education and Science. Thus the influence of the Schools Council would spread far and wide throughout the country. This certainly happened and most of the people concerned would, I think, agree that their period at the Schools Council influenced their beliefs and their future hopefully for the better. Such a structure and such an administration and such an atmosphere seems almost unreal in the harsher realities of the 1980s.

The Council has been criticized, often in my view unfairly, for its bureaucratic structure, for its irresponsibility, for its lack of impact in the school situation, and for its lack of success in reform in the examination field. The device that I have mentioned of change at the top did not stop the organization from becoming middle-aged as all organizations must. But I do not wish to apologize for my work in those days. I believe that many of the curriculum innovations were of great importance and that we have not yet seen the full fruits of those innovations. My confession under this heading is a rather proud statement, certainly not an apology. *I was a Wet in the Schools Council.*

My next confession is really related to the title that I held for eight years as Professor of Curriculum Research and Development. I never liked it and I never really understood what the phrase 'Curriculum Research and Development' meant. The Council at that time was occupied in large-scale development. It was not much interested in careful, cool, psychometric type research of the kind I had practised in the past. Hence there was a need to adopt a different style of research. The concept 'research and development' was taken over from engineering and it was immediately apparent to me that in the field of curriculum innovation the concept needed considerable modification. The development phase more often than not did not follow from a particular research phase. So I conceived the idea that in education, research and development should interact with each other, that in some projects the development would begin first based upon hunches, ideas, ideals, and thoughts of creative people. Very often such a development would throw up problems which would themselves call for careful research so that in some cases we would begin with the development aspect and eventually carry out research projects. In some others we would start with research and continue with development in the more orthodox engineering manner. Similarly with regard to evaluation it was very clear to me that the Council committees, and indeed the mood of the whole nation, at that time, was not seeking for elaborate independent evaluations of the curriculum innovations being planned. Rather there was the need for ongoing or formative evaluations rather than final or summative ones. So we created a group of critical friends, we appointed to most of the projects an evaluator who would not pretend to be independent of the project but sympathetic to it, would organize the feedback from the curriculum development projects in such a way as to make them more efficient. He or she would ask crucial questions of the developers. The other phrase coined in those days, by Parlett and Hamilton, was 'illuminative evaluation'. All those working in this mode were impatient with the more orthodox evaluation procedures, recognized that such work was inappropriate in the rough and ready situation ensuing from most curriculum innovation. Perhaps this led to a certain lack of theory and to a certain amount of, perhaps slip shod is too strong a phrase, lack of consideration of the finer details of possible planning. Certainly I have always remained critical of most aspects of curriculum theory. I once went to the United States and was interested to learn of a meeting of Professors of Curriculum Theory. I went to the meeting in an attempt to discover what I thought might be an unusual animal. I was sadly disappointed. I heard little theory which seemed to me in the slightest bit profound, and my colleagues at the meeting seemed very ordinary human beings. Curriculum theory has produced a number of models of the curriculum but I am afraid I am unrepentant in believing that most curriculum theory of this kind is very arid. In so far as we need theory, and we certainly do, it will come to us from psychology, sociology and philosophy and also from the curriculum aspects of the subjects of the curriculum themselves. I find similar difficulties in planning for courses in the university of an advanced kind under the heading of curriculum studies or curriculum development. I find myself unsympathetic to many of the so-called models of the curriculum. When curriculum development was invented in the 1960s it did not mean that curriculum studies had not taken place in the past and now as curriculum development becomes less fashionable so it does not mean that curriculum studies and curriculum innovation will not continue into the 1980s and the 1990s. Perhaps my confession under this heading should not simply be that I did not like the title curriculum research and development but that I did not appreciate even what the Curriculum Study Group meant. Like the man who had been speaking prose all his life without knowing it, many conducted curriculum studies in the 1940s and the 1950s before the phrase was invented and others will continue to do so in the 1980s and 1990s even if curriculum development as an activity become less fashionable.

Most of my confessions so far have a touch of arrogance about them. They are not really confessions, they are simply statements with which I hope you will agree. But the next one has an element, I think, of contrition in it. It's made not only on my behalf but on behalf of many others working in the field of curriculum development in the 1960s and early 1970s. I think we were all slow to see the defects of the systems that I have outlined. We were very confident. We thought that we would avoid in England the mistakes made in other parts of the world, particularly in the United States where the failure of large scale curriculum development became evident at an early stage. We felt that by keeping our feet on the ground, by organizing feedback, by using formative evaluation, by making sure that the work was done throughout the country in various local institutions that we should avoid the airy fairy nature of certain kinds of innovation. We were slow to see the abiding difficulty of effective innovation. We felt that by having teacher control of the Schools Council committees we had solved the question of participation. This is, of course, not so. A teacher is likely to be more sympathetic to an innovation if he or she participates.

So the question of the dissemination and implementation of the large curriculum development projects was recognized rather slowly and even when the problems were recognized the solutions have proved to be very difficult. It has become clear that before innovations will be accepted in practice in the schools, the teachers concerned will need to be involved, will need to have the support of their colleagues, and will need to feel that they have adequate resources. The research and development movement took some time before it became the research development and dissemination movement.

A few years ago I edited a book on the problems of dissemination in Europe in which it became clear that the problems we were encountering in this country were shared throughout Europe, whatever the educational system. Let us take one particular example — it was just as difficult in France with its centralized system to make sure that the teachers carry out the intentions of the central authorities as it was in more diffuse and diverse systems. In all kinds of educational systems the teacher will not carry out innovations unless he or she is convinced of their wisdom and is fully confident of his ability to implement them in the classroom situation. I think I was slow to see the immense problems associated with dissemination and particularly the need to carry the local education authority with the national body on such enterprises. This I suspect was one of the chief changes in the reorganization of the Schools Council. Now the local education authorities themselves have much more influence and will not allow innovations to take place unless they are confident that they can provide the resources within the locality to make such innovations possible.

My next confession is in some ways the most bitter of all from the point of view of the future. The difficulties involved in dissemination led us to see the importance of teacher participation in any proposed innovation. Hence the next phase of curriculum development should take place at local level and it should be associated with the in-service training of teachers, preferably in a school-based situation. So the need was for more local work, more INSET and for less large scale developments. At this point Eric Briault, late Education Officer for the Inner London Education Authority, stated, with frightening clarity, a paradox which went something like this 'we can see the need for local curriculum development but we cannot see why local money should be provided for a national organization such as the Schools Council to plan local work back in the local education authority itself'. Why should the local education authority provide money for work it could well do itself? This is a nasty paradox for a national organization. The chief answer must be that there is within the national body a somewhat superior wisdom from that which can be gleaned in the local education authority itself. The bigger that authority the more reluctant are the local people to agree with such a suggestion. My confession is that as a Schools Council man I could never see any solution to that question and my worry is that I still cannot see any adequate answer.

My seventh confession can be dealt with quite briefly. It is concerned with the current argument with regard to a core curriculum, its importance, relevance and necessity in the present situation. I am an unrepentant and strong critic of those people who advocate such a core curriculum and I have written on the issue in the second number of the Journal *Curriculum*. I shall, therefore, only briefly say here that my chief worry about arguments in favour of a common core curriculum is that if the proposals are produced in any detail then there is a grave danger that what is described as a minimum may turn out to be a maximum. Secondly, I do not believe that curriculum planners take enough notice of the problem of individual differences, particularly in these days with comprehensive schooling in our secondary educational system. It must be obvious to everybody that the range of ability from the very brightest to the dullest is extremely great and that if such a range is present within any one class the idea of a common minimum core is almost meaningless. If, as in the recent curriculum documents the prescriptions for a common core are put forward in a highly generalized way, then I'd submit that the generalization is such as to be comparatively useless. What I do think is important is to reduce the number of options available in our current examinations procedures. We do have too many choices for the various 16+ and 18+ examination syllabuses, but that is another matter which I'll take up in a few moments. Suffice it to say at the present time that my seventh confession is that I do not believe in the idea of a core curriculum. I am however encouraged by the Schools Council publication *The Practical Curriculum* which is a great improvement on the DES document.

My eighth point is not so much in the form of a confession at all but more in a statement that in the early days of the Schools Council my colleagues were slow to recognize the importance of the teaching aspects involved in curriculum development. To listen to many curriculum developers one would almost think that the methods of teaching and the way in which the subject matter is taught was unimportant. I do not suppose that my colleagues mean it to be like that, but nevertheless in many of the discussions of curriculum issues the teaching methods aspect is minimal. Perhaps the reason for this is the difficulty involved in prescribing for teachers the best methods of teaching. In a sense the early curriculum developers deliberately ignored some of the important problems associated with teaching method though the Humanities Curriculum Project helped changed this situation. Perhaps these problems are intractable, perhaps it was a sensible thing for a number of years to concentrate on the curriculum innovations themselves, ignoring problems of individual differences and ignoring the vital questions of how the curriculum should be taught.

Certainly in the Schools Council in the early days there was a deliberate avoidance of the normal institutions dealing with teacher training — the colleges of education and the university departments of education. The normal network of curriculum development went from the Department of Education and Science itself via the local education authorities, via the teachers' centres, which were a new invention in the Schools Council, and hopefully to the teacher in the classroom. The teacher training institutions were deliberately ignored. That this was a folly was obvious to me from the start and I spent a good deal of my time in the early days of the Schools Council advocating the involvement of the teacher trainers. Not everybody fell into the trap that I am now describing and the best example of a success story in this situation was the work in the 1960s and 1970s with regard to primary mathematics. Here there was an interesting combination of conventional curriculum development procedures, as exemplified in the Nuffield Primary Maths Project. But this was combined with the very impressive work carried out in terms of changing the primary arithmetic curriculum into a mathematics curriculum best exemplified by the work of Edith Biggs, Staff Inspector for Mathematics. She conducted a number of workshops throughout the country, first of all deliberately working with the teacher training colleges and with the university departments of education on the principle that the young potential teachers were the carriers of innovation. Both procedures are surely necessary. The change which was certainly effective in mathematics teaching in the primary school is a good example of the value of the interaction of conventional curriculum development methods with the training and influence and capture of the minds of the young teachers. INSET for experienced middle-aged teachers is however an equally vital necessity for the future health of education in this country. The full integration of in-service work with curriculum development work is still not achieved in this country. It is extraordinary to think that in the early days of the Schools Council they were specifically refused the right to consider in-service training in any generality. Only if the in-service work impinged directly on curriculum development were the Schools Council allowed to be involved in any direct way. This seems an absolute nonsense in the present day. I can put this aspect of my talk into a confession best by relating the first question asked of me when I was interviewed for the Chair in Curriculum Research and Development at the University of Reading.

'May I ask Professor Wrigley an idiot boy question. Surely amidst all these curriculum matters what really is of importance is how the topic is taught.' My confession is that whilst agreeing with the question I fear that I gave an inadequate answer.

My ninth confession is in some ways the most painful. Whilst proud of some of my work on the reform of the examination system I am disappointed with the general outcome and pessimistic with regard to the future of the common examination system. I suppose you could have really called me an examination man rather than a curriculum man as I owe a good deal in my career to my work in the examination field. I have already referred to the work of the Curriculum Study Group in terms of planning the Certificate of Secondary Education. At that time I played a leading part in the creation of the CSE arguing the necessity for teacher control, for the need for examinations to follow the curriculum, for the necessity of mode 3 examination procedures, for the need to release teaching and the curriculum from the tyranny of examinations. This was an important philosophy shared with many members of Her Majesty's Inspectorate and brought to an interesting fruition in the CSE and particularly in the mode 3 procedures. The arguments involved seemed in retrospect to be comparatively easy. The CSE was set up in a short period of years designed as it was for children of lesser ability than those taking GCE 'O' level. It seemed important that the best of the work in the secondary modern schools should not be hampered by conventional examinations and there was throughout the country a remarkable agreement on the need for a new examination. Many enlightened educationalists needed persuasion but I found it relatively easy to persuade them, employing arguments to do with the artificiality of normal examinations procedures and the need for a different system, a system which would rely upon the knowledge and expertise of the teacher to define standards and to make sure that the examination syllabus and the examination procedures would be put second to the curriculum itself. It was an exciting time. The CSE was created, developed and implemented in a remarkably short period. After that the situation seems to have got very much more difficult. In the first week of my taking up my appointment with the Schools Council in September or October 1967 I took part in a meeting designed to investigate the possibility of a common system of examining at 16+. A measure of the difficulty of reform in examinations is that, seventeen years later a common system is not yet implemented although agreed; it may be with us by 1990. Even more dispiriting is the outcome of the work in the Schools Council and in other places of the possible reform of the 18+ system. The arguments involving the sixth-form curriculum are truly educational and less concerned with the question of assessment. Yet throughout the years beginning with the Butler-Briault proposals, the N and F proposals, and the latest compromise in the situation, reform in the sense of broadening the sixth form curriculum has defeated all the innovators. The proposed new as level is a modest improvement but it is uncomfortably similar to the old Subsidiary Higher School Certificate examination that I took forty years ago. To look back over such work as has been done is to be somewhat discouraged. The arguments have often been false, ranging around the question of the reduction of standards and ignoring the important curriculum aspects of the broadening of the syllabuses. My actual confession though takes even me by surprise! I find myself independently in agreement with an Ex-Chairman of the Schools Council, John Tomlinson, in thinking that the right solution for the future is the abolition in its entirety of examining at 16+. It is, of course, perfectly possible, and indeed logical, to devise an examination instrument which will measure over the whole range of ability or even from the fortieth to the hundredth per centile in terms of ability. One of the chief defects of the GCE and CSE system has been with regard to dual entry and the immense problems arising from having two examinations overlapping each other. The logic of all that, is, of course, to produce a common system. It is then necessary either to have a complicated system of overlap of papers or else to design common examination papers for a wide range of ability. My prediction is that if and when we achieve a common system, and if and when we achieve common examination papers, we shall not like them. It seems to me in retrospect that the crucial change came when the school leaving age was raised to 16 and for the first time the public examination system at 16+ coincided with the leaving date. Before that time it was possible to argue that the examination system provided an important carrot to entice pupils to stay on at school. But now the future seems to me to lie in the field of profile reporting and results of school work which is by teachers themselves. I find it an interesting phenomenon that such different people as Harry Judge, the Director of the Oxford Department of Education, John Tomlinson, an ex-Chairman of the Schools Council and myself have apparently independently come to the same conclusion. *So my ninth confession is a painful one that much of the work (but not that on the CSE!) on examinations has either been unfruitful or somewhat misguided.*

My last confession is a rather arrogant one I fear and that is that I remain somewhat unrepentant. Perhaps most confessors are in this state though whether they should be at the moment that they make their confession is a debatable point which I will leave to the moral philosophers. I would, however, like to end on a positive note and to look forward to the future and to try to sketch out some of the points involved in curriculum innovation for the future. We still need, perhaps in a different guise the enthusiasm, insight and imagination of people like Derek Morrell. I sometimes wonder where are the equivalents of the imaginative civil servants of the past today. Are they ham-strung by the need for economy, by the present fashion for accountability and for saving money? Curriculum innovation will always be necessary. We are all, especially teachers, notably conservative, sometimes justifiably so, but not always. As teachers we tend to try out a method, revise it if it is somewhat unsuccessful and keep it as soon as it is reasonably successful. We become secure in our classrooms, in our conservative methods and are reluctant to change. So curriculum innovation will always be necessary. Take two obvious important innovatory situations which must be dealt with in the next few years. The first is the advent of micro-computers. Micro-computers will revolutionize the teaching methods used in this country in both primary and secondary schools. Is this a bold claim? Is it arrant nonsense? Is it destined to be proved wrong in the same way that those people in the past who advocated that television, radio, programmed learning would change the classroom out of all recognition? My hunch is that with micro-computers we really are in a new situation and that our teaching methods and our curriculum will be revolutionized. It is not just a question of using such instruments for computing purposes and for mathematics. Used correctly micro-computers will change the way in which we teach many other subjects than mathematics. In fact in considering our approach to the use of micro-computers I am struck by the way in which we are in a very similar situation to that of the early days of curriculum development. What seems to be needed is a development rather than a research process. The teachers themselves, in association with the children, who are, of course, remarkably adept in using new technology, will determine for themselves the new style of teaching and the new curriculum. An overplanned, over-organized research programme would be comparatively inappropriate but research problems may well arise as a result of the flooding of the market. It will not be long before there are micro-computers in every school and not long before these are being used by the majority of teachers. As this point research topics may arise so we are again in a very similar situation to the one I mentioned at the beginning whereby research and development do not follow in a logical process. The development may well come first and research second. The other place in which we can see the need for radical change is to do with the curriculum in the comprehensive school. Many aspects of the present academic curriculum derived from the old grammar schools can be seen to be relatively unimportant and inappropriate for future living. We need to plan a radical curriculum appropriate to the twenty-first century in a situation where mankind has more leisure, where we need to prepare people for a flexible living style, where new skills are necessary and where the old skills may be inappropriate. We have hardly begun to plan this new curriculum. In doing so many methods we have used in the past will surely be appropriate again.

The present stress on economy throughout the nation is particularly unfortunate in its effects upon the education system. I should like to make a point that although the swinging 1960s seem to be so attractive and although there seemed to be money for large-scale curriculum development and although the atmosphere in which we worked was one of trust, I would claim that money was not wasted and that in striving for economies and for more accountability we may well run into an extremely unimaginative system for the future. The best example of a problem which could be an opportunity is concerned with falling rolls in schools. For those of us who have lived through the days of shortage of teachers, of large classes, of inadequate resources, it is a tragedy to think that falling rolls are regarded as an immense problem rather than an opportunity. If only we were able to spend a fraction of the money which is wasted on other things as, for example, defence, we could transform the educational structure in this country. We spend pitiful amounts on research, on curriculum development, and on INSET, compared with the money we spend to defend an indefensible island. These words seem so inappropriate in the present climate of opinion and my stance seems to be unfashionable. It would convince Margaret Thatcher that I, indeed, was one of the Wets that I confessed to be. My slogan for the future is — *'better to be a militant Wet than a Wet militant'*.

[This paper was delivered as a lecture, and then printed in *Curriculum*, 4, 2. It is reprinted here with their kind permission]

Small r(esearch); big D(evelopment)

Freddie Sparrow

Other contributors to this volume will describe the changing political climate in which the Schools Council operated. This chapter will indicate something of the advantages and disadvantages, the stresses and reliefs, the sorrows and the joys of the Council staff. It might well be appropriate for me to do this as I had some twenty years of teaching in a wide variety of schools and nearly four years of research work at a University before I joined the Council, a background which gave me a teacher-researcher perspective on this remarkable institution. The political-institutional differentiation is somewhat artificial in that the atmosphere and ethos in which we worked changed as the political context changed, but it is valid in that the interaction between the two had profound effects on staff morale and efficiency. My particular role was concerned with research and evaluation and these brought me into regular contact with every aspect of the Council's work.

I was fortunate in joining in 1967 and so enjoyed those early years which Jack Wrigley has described as 'careless rapture'[1]. I was not aware of any euphoria — we were too busy for that — but there were many characteristics which made the place alive with genuine enthusiasm. One of the chief of these was the strong support of the DES and LEAs, not only in Committees and in the field, but also in the form of the secondment to the Council of first-class colleagues. The spirit was one of happy cooperation and dedication to causes, the intrinsic value of which nobody doubted. The top administrators were remarkable men. They were definitely in charge, but they exercised their power with a light touch and they never pretended omniscience. It was a daily occurrence for them to draw on the wide range of expertise and experience across the staff as a whole. We all recognised that 'the Council worked on the basis of a liberal philosophy of trust in the honesty and integrity of the individual'[2]. In this happy atmosphere individuals could exercise a great deal of freedom within the broad framework which everyone understood. The curricular priorities were fairly clear at this stage (preparing for RoSLA, the teaching of English and sixth-form examinations were typical examples). There were a number of research projects, many relating directly to the Mother Tongue, but all, including Enquiry 1,[3] relating specifically to the issues and problems of curriculum development. At this time it was assumed by all who sought to mount projects for the Council and by the decision-makers that everything we undertook would include an evaluation component. It was also at this time that the evaluators of Council projects began to meet regularly together and out of this cross-fertilization arose not only a number of books which made a considerable contribution to knowledge, but also a distinctive Council style of evaluation, based largely on the 'critical friend' concept, involving rigid adherence to no one particular model but selection, rather, from available methods — what a research colleague later called 'eclectic evaluation'. In retrospect I realize that our chief error in those days was the common assumption that the end product of projects must always be published materials, but this was an error we shared with most of the rest of the world. We did not, however, share with others a formal following of the 'Research, Development and Diffusion Model', which seemed to many of us to owe more to engineering than to the reality of the educational scene. Similarly we did not impose any rigid adherence to the formal behavioural objectives model, although we recognized that it was relevant, or partially relevant, in some areas of work. I tended to lose sympathy with it after its mechanistic and manipulative nature was demonstrated to me by one of its disciples who tried to insist on Overall Behavioural Objectives, Stagewise Behavioural Objectives, Subjectwise Behavioural Objectives, Unitwise Behavioural Objectives and Periodwise Behavioural Objectives. Ever since then the letters 'BO' have been expecially offensive to me!

The 'early years' period did not end suddenly; indeed many of its better qualities persisted in spite of difficulties throughout the Council's life. The first signs of change were not political, or, at least, not overtly so. As the original programme of work drew to a close a major problem was the formulation of a policy for the future. Some committee members thought that such a policy was in fact arrived at, but if this were so, it was very hard to discern. The main difficulty was that demands were numerous and resources limited. Among the areas which had not been included in the early work were the particular needs of the primary school sector, the creative arts, the arts subjects as a whole and the various sections of 'special' education. All these and many others had their advocates and in the circumstances the Council seemed to follow what might have been the only practical course — an ad hoc procedure based partly on perceptions of need and partly on the quality of the proposals received. This raised problems for the staff. We were specifically asked not to act as 'Counsel for the Defence' in presenting those proposals for which we were responsible at the processing stage, but this was interpreted with lattitude in some cases. We were also explicitly forbidden to inform proposers whose work had been rejected about the detailed reasons for rejection. This was understandable, but it inevitably caused some resentment, especially among the most enthusiastic proposers. I even heard a rumour that some people had concocted a league table of staff based on their alleged 'success' rate!

Another problem which affected chiefly the research staff was that out of the 'rag bag' of proposals came a rash of small projects, many of them staffed by a one or two man team. This seriously limited the possibilities of any proper evaluation. The research team did what it could and some of the solo workers on projects covered what they could of the evaluation field, but the main emphasis was placed more and more on the 'development' phase and even this often went agley because there was no flexibility in the small team to prevent failures to meet deadlines. Many people, including Geoffrey Cockerill, saw that there was a strong case for consolidation rather than continued expansion. I agreed with him, but at the same time I realized, as I'm sure he did, that if an organization includes in its structure a very wide range of teacher interests, all educationally valid, a very wide range of projects is certain to emerge. In retrospect I suspect that the Council at this stage had to offend either its constituent members or the DES.

At about the same time as this quandary arose it also became clear that the Council was not making the impact on the educational system which had tended to be taken for granted in the early years. The result was a period of intense questioning, starting with a working party on dissemination and continuing into the 'Impact and Take-up' project. Much of the blame was commonly held to be weaknesses in information channels and a survey I undertook on the distribution and use of the Council magazine 'Dialogue' certainly revealed a distressing lack of contact and an undoubted waste of money. The new Information Centres at Newcastle, Wakefield and Cardiff did a lot of good, but their opening coincided with a period of growing financial stringency in which schools experienced great difficulty in taking on new work. The Field Officer team, enlarged to provide more effective coverage of the country, worked minor miracles, but it soon became clear that the malaise was not amenable to piecemeal remedies. It would be an exaggeration to say that there was despondency and gloom among the staff, but there was most assuredly some despair when one of the main reasons for the Council's limited success was pointedly ignored. This reason was the over-concentration on the production of published materials. A further consideration of this will illustrate one of the basic weaknesses of the Council, one which contributed to its eventual demise.

Evidence of the serious limitations of published materials in the process of curriculum development derives from many sources. Most countries seem to have assumed initially that if they based their work where relevant on appropriate research, monitored their development work, modified it in the light of feed-back, then published the resultant materials, all would be well. Teachers, aware that some fellow teachers had been involved in the development, would buy the material, implement it, applaud the sponsoring agency and the curriculum development movement would have succeeded. In common with many others, I fell for this at first, but after only a short time I realized how naive it was. We knew from the work on the dissemination of curriculum development in Europe[4] that the issues involved were complex indeed. In no single one of the six countries studied was the mere production and availability of materials an answer and this was true, perhaps even more especially true, of countries like France which are known for their strongly centralized system of education. The same message came from the United States. John Goodlad of UCLA admits that he assumed that the many years of work on the curriculum and the many millions of dollars spent on materials had led to dramatic changes in schools. However, when he and his students actually went into the schools they discovered that in virtually every case the much lauded curriculum development movement had been a non-event.[5] As this sort of evidence accumulated I went back to the Lockwood Report to see if the document which led to the formation of the Schools Council was in any way to blame. I should have known better, as I knew of Derek Morrell's part in the Report. I found 'schools should . . . have responsibility for their own curricula and teaching methods, which should be evolved by their own staff to meet the needs of their own pupils'[6]. If Derek had lived he would surely have been saddened by all the emphasis placed on materials provided externally to the school, with none of the evolution deriving from the staff. Evidence of the same kind arose spontaneously at almost every meeting of the evaluators' group, but I must stress that I never heard any criticism of any commercial publishing house: it was the Council's publication policy which was the object of almost universal condemnation. The evaluators were not indulging in idle polemics; they, and I include the many project directors who attended the group meetings, were busy at the sharp end of curriculum development and they raised a myriad of studied criticisms. A typical example was Wynne Harlen's crucial point 'What teachers are required to do is to react to a ready-made package of problems which they may not have'[7].

Negative criticism is, of course, facile and commonly unproductive. There were, however, pointers to an alternative way of working, not as a substitute for the old, but as a constructive addition running in parallel with it. This has never been better expressed than by Wynne Harlen:

> But do glossy books and professionally produced packages extend an invitation for teachers to adapt, extend, criticize? Teachers would be more likely to do this if the materials did not give the impression of having finished the job, leaving nothing for others to do. Perhaps a less finished, less expensive form of product, including teachers' criticism of the content, would be a more direct invitation to other teachers to try out ideas experimentally rather than accept or reject them without modification. Being cheaper, these less finished products would at the same time be a better way to extend the range of choice open to teachers.[8]

The validity of this sort of comment is apparent, but we simply could not get the message across to the management of the day. We pointed out that curriculum development is a process rather than a package. We insisted, rightly in my view, that real curriculum progress is dependent on the professional growth of teachers. We pointed to the growing acceptance of the prime importance of in-service training. We pointed to the efforts of those who were working WITH teachers instead of presenting them with some sort of identikit product. We even ran a well-attended meeting of experienced and competent people in order to unravel some of the many problems attendant upon a more complex way of working. It was tragic indeed that these ideas were never even put to Council committees. Staff were, in effect, told that failure to venerate perfection of publication rather than practical service to teachers was a form of heresy, just as to articulate one's doubts was a form of blasphemy. Such a situation could not have arisen under the original regime. I remember Geoffrey Caston's comment when he was asked about the sense of comradeship and cooperation in the Council staff. 'It doesn't just happen, you know. You have to work at it all the time'. Under that regime the staff would have been encouraged to develop Wynne's ideas further, which might have led to something like this outline programme.

In carefully selected cases, as soon as materials were in rudimentary but useful form, they would be made available free of charge to teachers apart from photocopying costs. This could operate only with the blessing of LEAs, LEA advisers and Teachers' Centre Wardens. Help from university departments, colleges of education staff and HMI would have been invaluable. The only obligation on teachers, or preferably, groups of teachers, would be a request that they report either in writing or orally on outcomes. If the materials had no value, why not? Was there a lack of need? Was it too difficult/easy/ irrelevant? Would its use disrupt the class? Were other teachers opposed to its use? Was the school unable to accommodate the work within its timetable or general policy? What modifications would make the materials better? What were the reactions of the children? and so on. It is really quite astonishing that the Council never made any serious enquiry of teachers into those aspects of curriculum development in schools, ignorance of which was surely one cause of the Council's limited impact. A programme like this would have taken development out of the hot-house atmosphere of the traditional trial schools. It would have been untidy, messy perhaps, but it would have involved the people who really matter and even limited success would have provided the Council with such grass roots support as might have enabled it to survive. At the same time, it would have gone a long way towards an answer to what Jack Wrigley called 'the Briault paradox':

> We can see the need for local curriculum development but we cannot see why local money should be provided for a national organisation such as the Schools Council to plan local work back in the Local Education Authority itself. Why should the Local Education Authority provide money for work it could well do itself?[9]

The scheme outlined above would not have 'planned' local work — it would merely have made outline materials available only for those who wanted them. The method of use, the adaptations, the extensions in the light of local needs and even the rejection of the materials would have been entirely the business of the local school, division (where applic-able) or education authority. However, the existence of a national organization serving *all* LEAs would have gone some way to solving the age-old problem of inter-Authority communication and cross-fertilization. At the same time the accumulation of information about the many variations in schools and classrooms, teachers' attitudes, the teaching and learning milieu, the facilitators and inhibitors of curriculum change, in fact much of what Cremin meant by 'the ecology of education'[10] would have become available for all who wanted or needed to comprehend fundamental curricular issues.

Many, perhaps most, of the Council staff frequently felt frustrated, bitter or simply furious at their inability to do anything about intransigent attitudes. Most gave up trying. One told me 'I find that banging my head against a brick wall hurts, so I'm giving up'. The idea of going directly to committee members, many of whom would almost certainly have been sympathetic, was tempting but unacceptable. We knew that the house was united in most respects and hoped that the one sense in which it was divided would disappear in time. Moreover, the Council was facing serious threats and it seemed worthwhile to maintain a level of unity, the better to face the challenge.

Much of the criticism levelled at the Council was ill-informed. It presented the institution with a familiar problem: 'Do we ignore, thereby implying a plea of 'Guilty', or do we, by responding, elevate the status of the critics and give an impression of special pleading?' The staff provided information as requested and left the task of responding to the Chairman. We were fortunate in that the last three Chairmen were of so high a calibre that if they could not save the Council, nobody could. Each is contributing to this volume, but as all contributors have been asked for 'a vigorous personal statement', I will comply in the form of brief comments on some matters of interest and concern to me personally, such as the examinations issues; the changing attitude of the DES; the constitutional review and the change in style from projects to programmes.

I came into educational research on the assessment side, spent much of my early service on examinations work and retained a deep interest throughout my tenure at the Council. Of all the innumerable questions which merit consideration, that which in retrospect most intrigues me is the contrast between the Council and its examinations predecessor, the Secondary Schools Examinations Council. They had in common the devoted service of high-minded and competent people, but whereas the SSEC reported to the Ministry (which seems normally to have accepted its recommendations), the Council kept the DES informed through its participation in committees, but submitted its recommendations to all the interested parties, including the universities and the teachers (who seem normally to have rejected them)! Many of the SSEC ideas were later rescinded — the age 16 limit on 'O' level entry is an example. The Council's ideas were never implemented. It is strange that all knowledgeable people agree that changes in the examination structure are urgently needed, but they simply cannot agree on the form they should take. The SSEC never attracted public or widespread criticism. The Council became a focal point of attack, largely because it 'went public'. On one occasion I met hostility from a teacher who accused the Council of changing the system to which he had grown accustomed and he wished to remain unchanged. I asked him if he knew that the proposed changes were recommended by the representatives of his own professional association. Had he written, or did he now intend to write, to voice his anxieties in the appropriate place? He had the grace to look abashed, but the incident is typical of the way damage can be done. No doubt there are other areas in which some of the mud which should never have been thrown has tended to stick!

A gradual change in the attitude of the DES towards the Council was apparent to most of the staff. One of its early manifestations was a reduction in the number of HMIs seconded to the Council and eventually their total withdrawal. This was a great disappointment to us all and I was especially sorry to lose the valued regular cooperation with people who really knew from experience in schools a great deal about the realities of the educational world. They also had the great advantage over most of the rest of the staff that they enjoyed security of tenure in the Inspectorate and could thus exercise a degree of independence of attitude and opinion denied to most of us. They were, of course, always discreet, but I knew from many conversations that the objectivity of their outlook was of great value to the Council. At about the same time as HMIs were withdrawn, the Council suffered its cruellest blow. A DES document was 'leaked'. It revealed that the Department, or some of its members, were condemnatory of the Council's work, some of which was held to be 'mediocre'. The staff accepted without question that anyone has an absolute right to criticize anything, but what perplexed them was the fact that in this case the critics were included in the membership of committees and were thus in part responsible, if only by failure to express their views honestly in the appropriate context, for the very work they now criticized. In this difficult situation the staff were grateful indeed for all Sir Alex Smith's efforts on the Council's behalf.

The constitutional review and the resulting new Council structure would make a fertile source for a detailed study of institutions. The idea, for instance, of replacing the former Governing Council (which never really governed!) and the Programme Committee with three new bodies, a Convocation, a Finance and Priorities Committee and a Professional Committee illustrated one of the most interesting characteristics of education. It is the odd man out of the various areas of human activity which have to use qualified and experienced profession-als. If we need legal help we go to a lawyer; medical help to a doctor; help with accounts, to an accountant; help with house design, to an architect, and so on. In every such case we accept our limited personal knowledge of the field and our resultant dependence on the experts. However, one has only to be mildly interested in the matter of teaching and learning to discover that almost everybody is an expert in educa-tion. In most cases this is, of course, self-delusion, but in the case of the membership of Convocation there was some truth in it. In this 'Education Parliament' there was a range of interests and talents the like of which had probably never before assembled together. It was demo-cratic in a sense that a government department never can be and this, together with the obvious embarrassment of most of the DES repre-sentatives who attended its meetings, must have aroused antagonism and resentment. Another result of the 'odd man out' syndrome was that every attempt to reduce the total number of committees in the new structure failed so badly that in the end the number was increased. In order to become more democratic, the Council actually became more bureaucratic, more expensive to administer and even more diffuse in its new policies. The change from projects to programmes was entirely laudable in its intent, but the total ground which the Council attempted to cover was so wide as to make detailed work in each segment virtually impossible, and so varied in its nature as to limit severely the effective-ness of any evaluation of it.

This chapter began with an indication of the goodwill, the coopera-tion and the friendliness of the early years of the Council's life. Perhaps one of the most astonishing truths of the Council is that, in spite of all the slings and arrows, in spite of the failures I have indicated and in spite of the feeling that, come Trenaman, come programmes, come anything, the powers that be would close the institution down, most of the staff retained that esprit de corps, that mutual respect and affection and that conviction that, despite everything, the ideals of the Council were worth striving to attain. The kindnesses we enjoyed were too numerous to count. The friendships we made were deep and lasting. The contribu-tions we made were hopefully not all 'writ in water'. One day, maybe, a new Schools Council will rise, Phoenix-like, from the ashes and maybe it will learn from the minor failings and benefit from the many successes of its predecessor.

Freddie Sparrow

Notes

1 WRIGLEY, J. (1983) 'Confessions of a curriculum man', *Curriculum*, Vol. 4, No. 2, and this volume.
2 *Ibid.*
3 Equiry 1: *The Young School Leaver (1968)*; A survey of attitudes of young people, their parents and teachers.
4 RUDDUCK, J. and KELLY, P. (1976) *The Dissemination of Curriculum Development* a European Trend Report, NFER Publishing Co. for the Council of Europe.
5 GOODLAD, J.T. (1978) 'What schools are for: an American perspective on the Green Paper', *Trends in Education*, DES.
6 LOCKWOOD, J. (1964) *Report of the Working Party on the Schools' Curricula and Examinations.*
7 HARLEN, W. (1979) 'Curriculum evaluation' in TAYLOR, P.H. and RICHARDS, C. *An Introduction to Curriculum Studies*, NFER.
8 *Ibid.*
9 WRIGLEY, J. (1983) *op. cit.*
10 CREMIN, L.A. (1976) in *Public Education*, New York, Basic Books.

The Other Paymaster — the View from the Local Authorities

Eric Briault

In nearly all parts of the world, except in this country, schooling is under unified control, in some cases at a comparatively local level. School organisation, the provision of teaching staff and the content of the curriculum are settled by a single controlling authority. Our system of distributed control and administration is found hard to understand, confusing, hard to justify. The cooperation between the three partners — central government, local education authority and the teachers — easily becomes a triangle of tension and the history of curriculum control in England and Wales between the early sixties, before the Schools Council was set up, and the present time, when it has been demolished, reflects the varying strength, over that time, of the influence exercised by one or another of the partners. Statutorily, the local education authorities are responsible for the curriculum and central government for decisions about examinations. The close links between curriculum and examinations, at least at secondary school level, were reflected, organizationally for the first time, in the setting up of a council 'for the Curriculum and Examinations'. How did this come about?

Two originally quite separate developments form the background to the setting up of the Lockwood Committee and its recommendations for the formation of the Schools Council. The first was the mounting pressure from the LEAs and the teachers during the second half of the 1950s for a new examination below the level of the GCE to meet the needs of the increasing number of pupils in the secondary modern schools and the comprehensive schools who were staying on at school to 16 but for whom the GCE was too academic or too difficult. The pressure was orchestrated and largely brought to bear by Sir William Alexander (as he then was) the Secretary of the Association of Education Committees (AEC). The local authorities were associated with one another in two separate organizations, the County Councils' Association (CCA) and the Association of Metropolitan Authorities (AMA), as they are now: the AEC not only included all local *education* authorities except the London County Council (LCC), but also was unique in that the authorities were represented by both elected members and professioanl officers. Moreover, the AEC had much closer links with the teachers' organizations than either the CCA or the AMA. The reorganization of local government in 1974 saw the slaughter of the AEC by the other two associations, jealous of the power and influence of its Secretary, of its 'special pleading' for education and ill-content with its non-party political but largely professional stance. In the years preceding the formation of the Schools Council, the AEC, and in particular its Secretary, were most influential; and this influence, when conjoined with that of the National Union of Teachers (NUT) in particular and the teachers' associations generally, Ministers found hard to resist. The pressure brought to bear on ministers, who for years resisted the development of the new examination asked for, finally brought about the setting up of the Beloe Committee, the recommendation of a Certificate of Secondary Education and its acceptance by the Minister in 1961, as he said 'reluctantly'.

At about this time, the second development was beginning, namely a recognition within the Department of Education that there was a need for the curriculum in the schools to move with the times and for new initiatives to take place. Professor Gosden, to whose inaugural lecture in 1982 as Professor of the History of Education I am much indebted, stated in the course of the lecture:

> Now the events leading to the decision to establish the Certificate of Secondary Education took place against a background in which some of those in the Ministry were by this time feeling that they were ill-prepared to cope with developments. In an interesting internal paper on the work of Schools Branch written in 1961, it was stated that the function of LEAs was simply to secure that enough suitable schools were provided for their areas and to see they were effectively maintained. It was a function of the Minister to make and apply sound policies. This ought to include specifically educational policies, these being defined to cover teaching methods, subjects, curricula, examinations, the internal organization of schools and the use of staff within schools. Therefore there needed to be established within Schools Branch a policy-making organ for this purpose.

The organ should take the form of a full-time development group, to be headed jointly by a staff inspector and an assistant secretary. The group might consist of twelve to fifteen members drawn from the Inspectorate and from the Department. It could be organized into teams of three or four depending on the nature of the problems to be tackled.

The Beloe proposals for a CSE obviously needed to be worked on and developed before they could be put into practice and this seemed to present just the opportunity for the sort of thinking within the Ministry, represented by the Schools Branch paper, to come to fruition, at least in the field of curriculum and examinations. On 9 March 1962 Mary Smieton, by now Permanent Secretary, sent a letter to local authorities' and teachers' associations to let them know what was afoot. The Ministry was in the process of setting up a study group which would concern itself with the curriculum and examinations and with their administrative implications. The main job of the unit would be to improve the value of the service that the Inspectorate and the Department were able to offer in this area. She went on to explain that a team was going to be formed to deal with CSE examination matters and would be concerned with advising the SSEC and its committees. All were to understand that this would not change the functions or reponsibilities of the SSEC in any way; the new unit would merely be offering a service function. In a subsequent speech by the Minister, care was taken to reassure teachers and local authorities that the existing pattern of powers would not be disturbed in any way.[1]

It was not long, however, before the creation of the Curriculum Study Group was seen by the LEAs and the teachers to be a threat to their control of the curriculum and once more it was Alexander who expressed this fear, vehemently in private, strongly when AEC went on deputation to the Minister over the matter. Sir Ronald Gould, Secretary of the NUT, joined forces with Sir William, and Sir William Houghton, the London County Council Education Officer (to whom I was Deputy), lent his support. The outcome was a meeting in July 1963 with the Minister, Sir Edward Boyle, to which representatives of the LEAs and the teachers and certain other interested bodies were invited. Before this took place there had occurred an event of crucial importance for the eventual Schools Council. This was the transfer to the Schools Branch in the Ministry in early 1962 of a most remarkable civil servant, and his subsequent appointment as Joint Head of the Curriculum Study Group

(CSG), Derek Morrell. It was he who, in early 1963, had drafted a paper on a 'Proposed Schools Council for the Curriculum and Examinations', of which he sent a copy to Alexander.

Morrell was a dynamic, persuasive and far-seeing educational administrator. Pre-eminently Morrell recognized and believed deeply in three things: the need for curriculum innovation; the importance of the relationship between the curriculum and examinations; and the critical importance, in the English system of distributed administration and control of education, of cooperation between the three partners, the Department of Education, the LEAs and the teachers. The outcome of Boyle's meeting in July 1963 (tactfully held at Hamilton House, the NUT headquarters) was agreement to the setting up of a working party under the chairmanship of Sir John Lockwood with the following terms of reference:

> This representative meeting held in London on 19th July, 1963
>
> (a) notes there is wide support for the proposal to establish co-operative machinery in the fields of the school curriculum and examinations;
>
> (b) appoints a working party comprising, under the chairmanship of Sir John Lockwood, one representative of each of the bodies present at the meeting, together with assessors and a secretariat appointed by the Minister of Education, to consider how effect could best be given to the matters discussed and to make recommendations;
>
> (c) agrees to reconvene to consider and reach conclusions on the working party's recommendations.[2]

Morrell, Alexander and Gould agreed on the basic principles of the proposed Council; it was Morrell who redrafted his original proposals to make them more acceptable and Alexander who put them to the Lockwood Committee. While certainly the teachers, and for the most part the education administrators, were in favour of the proposals, elected members had their doubts and still feared central control or, at least, over much central influence, under cover of the proposed Council. Sir Ronald Gould recalls an invitation by Mrs. Marjorie McIntosh, Chairman of the LCC Education Committee, to himself and Sir William Houghton, at which Mrs. McIntosh pressed them to oppose the proposal, from which as he says, the visitors emerged 'like wet rags'! Mrs. McIntosh's objections were summarized in a memorandum included in the AEC archives from which I quote by kind permission of the Brotherton Library, University of Leeds:

Is the proposed Schools Council, serviced by the Ministry's Curriculum Study Group, a desirable development?

In my view, the proposal carries two possible dangers to the integrity of our educational tradition and thus to the health of a free society. In the first place, it will create conditions favourable to an increase in control by central government over the curriculum and methods of teaching. It can hardly fail to facilitate the emergence of text-books and other teaching materials which, despite the good intentions of the Curriculum Study Group and its collaborators will run serious risk of becoming or being regarded as 'official'. Secondly, the Schools Council could scarcely avoid being treated and accepted as the approved initiator of educational developments within its terms of reference despite the Ministry's intentions. Inevitably, the Curriculum Study Group will come to dominate the Schools Council as the Schools Council must come to dominate research. We may channel its resources to those persons and projects of which it approves. Approved research may become safe research which embarrasses no one. Such an outcome is inherent in the proposed constitution of the Council the secretariat of which is to be provided by the Curriculum Study Group.

Many of the proposed Council's functions properly belong to universities, to independent research organizations, to professional bodies and to local education authorities. Surely, tradition and experience alike require that it is the local authorities not the Curriculum Study Group which should 'provide arrangements such that the ideas of teachers can be tried out, developed, assessed' and made available to other teachers. The Schools Council is proposed as the 'framework within which it (the Curriculum Study Group) ought to operate'. The Group is a creation of the Ministry under the control of the Ministry which provides the framework within which it operates. It seems superfluous to establish a Schools Council in order to justify the existence of a Study Group already set up by the Ministry.[3]

On looking again at the Lockwood Report, I was surprised to find that I was the alternate member to Mrs. McIntosh. I was never called upon to attend. In the event, however, the fears expressed were evidently overcome and indeed proved in time to be groundless. The working party was able to submit an agreed report to the Minister in March 1964, the reconvened representative meeting agreed it in June and the Schools Council met in October 1964. Two themes stand out in the working party's report: the pre-eminence of the schools in determining curricula and the desire to achieve cooperation between the partners in the education service. Certain of the Lockwood conclusions are worth quoting, for they are under some challenge at the present time:

6   We noted that it has long been accepted in England and Wales that the schools should have the fullest possible measure of responsibility for their own work, including responsibility for their own curricula and teaching methods, which should be evolved by their own staff to meet the needs of their own pupils. We re-affirm the importance of this principle, and believe that positive action is needed to uphold it.

7   The responsibility of the individual schools for their own work is not, however, an exclusive responsibility. It has inevitably to be exercised within a wider framework which takes account of the general interest of the community, both local and national, in the educational process. Within this general framework, individual schools have to take a wide range of particular decisions on educational content and methods.

8   The work of the schools also has to be related to the requirements of the many and varied establishments of higher and further education to which many of the pupils will go on leaving school, and to the training arrangements and entry requirements of a wide range of professional bodies and of employers generally. There is thus a complicated, and constantly changing, relationship between the work of the schools and many particular outside interests.

9   The responsibility placed upon the schools is a heavy one. If it is to be successfully carried, the teachers must have adequate time and opportunity for regular re-appraisal of the content and methods of their work in the light of new knowledge, and of the changing needs of the pupils and of society. A sustained and planned programme of work is required, going well beyond what can be achieved by occasional conferences and courses, or by the thinking and writing of busy teachers in their spare time.

15   In short, our conclusions on the nature of the problem are as follows:

(1) The present arrangements for determining the curriculum in schools and the related examinations are not working well: in particular, teachers have insufficient scope for making or recommending modifications in the curriculum and examinations.

(2) Different arrangements are needed to achieve the balanced co-operation of the teachers, the Local Education Authorities, the Ministry of Education, the establishments of higher and further education, and others, in a continuing process of modifying the curriculum and examinations.

(3) More resources and more effort should be devoted to co-operative study, research and development in this field.

17 (2) The character of the new body should be that of a free association of equal partners who would combine to promote, through co-operative study of common problems, the pursuit of common objectives. The Schools Council would not, in other words, be advisory to the Minister of Education alone: it would be advisory to all its member interests. These interests would retain unimpaired their right to take decisions within their own areas of responsibility but they would seek, through the agency of the Schools Council, to co-ordinate their decisions in harmony one with another. Authorities and bodies in membership of the Council would, of course, be free to delegate such of their executive functions to the Council as they might consider desirable, just as the Minister now delegates to the Secondary School Examinations Council some of his functions as central co-ordinating authority for secondary school examinations. We would expect this particular arrangement to continue if and when a Schools Council for the Curriculum and Examinations were set up.

19 The objects of the Schools Council for the Curriculum and Examinations are to uphold and interpret the principle that each school should have the fullest possible measure of responsibility for its own work, with its own curriculum and teaching methods based on the needs of its own pupils and evolved by its own staff: and to seek, through co-

operative study of common problems, to assist all who have individual or joint responsibilities for, or in connection with, the schools' curricula and examinations to co-ordinate their actions in harmony with this principle.[4]

At the first meeting of the Schools Council, which I attended, Sir John Maud (as he then was), the first Chairman, announced the main areas of the curriculum to which the Council should address itself. I remember wondering at the time who invented them. Jos Owen, one of the first joint secretaries, along with Morrell and Robert Morris HMI, tells me:

> The earliest statement about the curriculum emerged from discussions between the joint secretaries and HMI. It was very much more a product of CSG than of any structured exchange with LEAs. Rather unusually, it was not entirely to do with Morrell. I remember especially the SI for English (Glyn Lewis) as well as Robert Morris making pointed contributions to the language and mathematics side. At the same time, I think that the connection with the Nuffield Foundation, and not least through Tony Becher, was fairly powerful.

Both in getting the agreement of the LEAs on the working party and in the early work of the Council, the role of the HMIs and their recognized independence was very important. Morris was succeeded as Joint Secretary by Robert Sibson. Unlike Ministry and LEA or teacher appointments to the triumvirate, who mostly stayed for two years or so, he remained in the post for seven years. No-one ever questioned his role or his independence of DES or political influence and his advice and accumulated wisdom was of great value to the Council.

The battles over the CSG were about the question 'who controls the curriculum?' The LEAs said firmly that the schools, that is the teachers do. But the teachers were rightly subject to powerful outside influences, whether or not the Minister (or now the Secretary of State) is seeking to be among them. The formation of the Schools Council depended on the proposition that the most important influences should be developed nationally and that major curriculum developments should be nationwide. This was already the case to some extent through the criticism and advice offered by HMIs and particularly through in-service courses for teachers mounted by HMIs. The Nuffield Foundation was funding several projects, of which Nuffield Science was to prove an outstanding example of this kind of development. The subject associations were another important source of influence on the curriculum, some much more active and effective than others, most of them, however, based strongly on the academic, subject specialist, grammar school tradition and feeling their way with varied success into curricula for the secondary modern and the comprehensive school. The attention they gave to the primary school varied from the considerable to the negligible. These influences were carried through into the Council's subject committees on which progressive teachers from the subject associations were, by one means or another, included in the membership. As the years went by, however, the teachers unions, especially the NUT, tended more and more to demand the right to fill places on the subject committees and did not always bring in the kinds of teachers who were most active in the subject associations. I would say, for example, that in the later years the Geographical Association, in which school teachers, teacher-trainers and university geographers were all active, was more influential than the Schools Council, even though there were one or two successful Council geography projects.

There remains a group of people who, in many but not all LEAs, exercised a powerful influence on curricular development in every sense — subject matter, teaching method, class organization. These were, and are, the LEAs' advisers and inspectors. At the time of the formation of the Schools Council, many authorities, particularly the counties, had only a few advisers and these in the specialist fields such as physical education, music and girls' and boys' (as they were in those days) crafts. On the other hand, many of the large urban authorities had larger and stronger groups of advisers, called in many cases, as they were in London, inspectors. I suppose my view of their influence is largely coloured by the power and prestige of the LCC/ILEA inspectorate (especially as I was a member of it from 1948 till 1956!). They were certainly in London a major means through which curriculum change occurred. The strength of their influence arose from several factors: they could be in regular touch with a range of teachers in the schools of the authority; they had access to or advised upon the allocation of additional resources; they directly advised and sometimes criticized teachers employed by their authority; and their advice carried considerable weight when teachers were appointed to headships, head of department posts and other above-scale positions. You have only to recall the work of Marion Richardson in art or Maisie Cobby in drama to illustrate the point. During the lifetime of the Schools Council, for example, the ILEA Staff Inspector for History enabled history teachers in the London comprehensive schools to develop an entirely new world history syllabus, which was widely taken up and strongly resourced by the schools themselves with the backing of the authority. The problems of dissemination were minimal compared with those which a Schools Council project faced. In recent years, curriculum development at the level of the individual LEA has grown steadily, authorities sending to all their schools 'guidelines' in maths, in science, in English and so on, in all cases developed by their own teachers, usually with some adviser/inspector input. Who is likely to ignore guidelines his or her employer sends out? Could it be that this development in part explains the absence of LEA opposition to the closure of the Schools Council?

The constitution of the Governing Council and the committee of the Schools Council reflected the principles which the Lockwood Committee adumbrated, quoted earlier, and led it to say 'we felt that it would be appropriate for a body described as a Schools Council for the Curriculum and Examinations to have a majority of members representing the schools and a substantial majority representing the schools together with other educational establishments'.[5] The eventual constitution followed the Lockwood recommendations closely, though not exactly. The Schools Council as at 31 December 1967, reported in the Council's first report: *The First Three Years* consisted, in addition to the Chairman, of fifty-nine members and ten coopted members. Twenty-five of the members were teachers representing the teachers' associations, all except two, schoolteachers, and of the ten cooptions, eight were teachers. As against this the LEAs had nine members and the DES four, two administrators and two HMIs. The three Steering Committees were equally dominated by the teachers, with fifteen or sixteen members, compared with which the local authority associations had five members in each case. (This was an advance on the three recommended by Lockwood). The Programme Committee, whose job it was 'to determine priorities in the use of the Schools Council's resources' again had to have a majority of teachers; the teacher associations had nine places and the local authorities three. Only on the Finance and Staff Committee were the teachers in a minority. Apart from this last Committee, I recall no occasion over the ten years during which I served on the Council and two of its major committees, when the LEA members acted as a group. Once appointed, each of us made his or her own contribution in a professional and certainly non-political way. On the other hand, the teachers, certainly the NUT, increasingly operated as a block, taking certain important decisions in a pre-meeting caucus. But many decisions were still taken at the Committee in the light of the discussion and the persuasive and knowledgeable could sometimes carry the day against a caucus vote. It was, I recall, hard to get the DES representatives to come out with a strong view or even an upheld hand.

I have long been fascinated with the art of committeemanship. Quite a lot can turn upon whom you sit next to. (Having been frequently placed as I have been, in another body, between Sir William Alexander and Max Morris, I am experienced in such things!) In the early days, except at the full Council meetings, one picked up one's name-card and chose one's seat though tacitly the block of seats for the NUT were inviolate. I would, if possible, choose a seat next to a colleague whose view I valued or whose support I wished to enlist. Of course, it was an entertainment in itself to sit next to Leslie Drew, who represented the AMC (as it then was, now the AMA). Another friendly neighbour was a university Vice-Chancellor whose expressions of view, especially on sixth-form matters, I found helpful. Sometimes one struck up an unholy alliance across the table with the National Association of Schoolmasters (NAS) against the NUT. Steering Committees spent a lot of time listening to proposals for new projects and discussing them after the proposers had retired. Officers developed subtle techniques in bringing these proposals forward and members, I like to think including myself, in eliciting information from the visitors which would be used — for or against — in the discussion after the proposers had gone. Despite these remarks about the constitution and behaviour of the committees, I am bound to say that by and large their activities reflected Morrell's original intention of cooperation between the partners in the education service and in a great many of the decisions about the Council's programme as it developed there was a reasonable consensus.

The LEA contribution to the work of the Council extended beyond that of their representatives on the Council and its committees by reason of LEA secondments to the Council's staff. Jos Owen, seconded from Somerset, was followed as Joint Secretary by Guy Rogers, at that time one of the ILEA District Inspectors. Immediately below this level were three 'Principals', two from the DES and one, Roy Price, an administrator seconded from the ILEA. Later on other authorities seconded officers, such as Tony Light, an adviser from Bristol who became a Joint Secretary in 1973. Local authority advisers/ inspectors also made important contributions to the subject committees, several of which were chaired by them, including two by ILEA inspectors. The ILEA Staff Inspector for Special Education chaired the working party in that field and Leslie Drew (at that time Director of Education, Swansea) the Working Party on the whole curriculum for 13–16 year old pupils. From time to time there were doubts about the three Joint-Secretaries arrangement and this was of course eventually changed. On reflection, I think on balance it was the right arrangement at least for the first few years, for it gave the partners in the enterprise a chance to share in the top posts and it avoided possible domination by a single personality. Senior Council staff coming from the LEAs operated in the same way as LEA representatives, that is to say they did their own professional thing. Part of the value of their contribution nevertheless was their local authority background, their 'feel' of the working of curriculum change in a single authority and of their association, whether as inspector, adviser or administrator, with teachers in the schools.

One other LEA contribution to the Council's work may be mentioned, namely providing house-room for individual projects. Some of us felt that the involvement of colleges of education in the work of the Council was too little and I was glad that the ILEA was able to accommodate the Stenhouse Humanities project at Philippa Fawcett College and the Geography for the Young School Leaver project at Avery Hill College.

I turn briefly to finance, the broad arrangements for which are well-known and upon which I have no comment. But I am quite sure that those of us who represented the LEAs felt a special obligation to try to make sure that the monies we (and the DES) were putting up for the Council were used wisely, effectively, economically and for the right purposes. Steering committees perhaps tended to give their blessing to all worthwhile projects and even to call for new ones in fresh areas. It was at the Programme Committee that the crunch came and here priorities had to be decided, for the budget could not carry all the possible runners. I like to think that LEA members of this Committee, such as myself and my then colleague, Bill Braide, who succeeded me, brought to bear on these discussions about priorities a down-to-earth and fairly sensitive appreciation of the needs of the schools and a pragmatic approach to costing and feasibility. There were however occasions when doubts arose. Perhaps I may quote Professor Jack Wrigley, Director of Studies with the Council (a joint appointment with the University of Reading) in a recent paper 'Confessions of a curriculum man'.

> My next confession is in some ways the most bitter of all from the point of view of the future of the Schools Council. The difficulties involved in dissemination led us to see the importance of teacher participation in any proposed innovation. Hence the next phase of curriculum development should take place at local level and it should be associated with the inservice training of teachers, preferably in a school based situation. So the need was for more local work, more Inset, and for less large scale developments. At this point Eric Briault, lately Chief Education

Officer for the Inner London Education Authority stated with frightening clarity a paradox which went something like this 'we can see the need for local curriculum development but we cannot see why local money should be provided for a national organization such as the Schools Council to plan local work back in the Local Education Authority itself'. Why should the Local Education Authority provide money for work it could well do itself? This is a nasty paradox for a national organisation. The chief answer must be that there is within the national body a somewhat superior wisdom from that which can be gleaned in the Local Education Authority itself. The bigger that authority the more reluctant are the local people to agree with such a suggestion. My confession is that as a Schools Council man I could never see any solution to that question and my worry is that on behalf of the Schools Council, an organisation which I would like to see flourish, I still cannot see any adequate answer.[6]

The dilemma arose in part from a certain disillusion with major projects which set in after the first eight or ten years and which led the Programme Committee to look favourably on smaller local projects and to offer pump-priming money for such developments. I took the line that unless there was really likely to be a spin-off at national level, I could not see why ILEA (for example) money which helped to pay for the Schools Council should be channelled back into another LEA for a project which might never surface outside that authority. I suppose it was a lot easier to take that line if you had the background of the enormous resources of the ILEA than if you were in a small and perhaps ungenerous authority. But the dilemma is more than a financial one, for it reflected the problem of the dissemination of national projects to which Professor Wrigley refers and to which I shall return later.

What of the other side of the Schools Council's responsibility, namely examinations? LEA representatives were as anxious as any, and a good deal more anxious than some, to make sense of the national pattern of examinations, for which of course the Secretary of State is ultimately responsible. The story is largely one of continuing frustration, save for the success of CSE in responding to the changing curricula of the secondary schools. The Examinations Committee was far too often the scene of battles between the GCE boards, defending their independence (they had teacher advisers but these were not representatively appointed), and the CSE boards, well and truly teacher controlled. In the experience of Bill Braide, a member, and sometime Vice-

Chairman, of the Metropolitan Regional Examination Board (Sir Harold Shearman was Chairman), the LEA input to the Board's activities was considerable and the help of the ILEA inspectorate, especially on subject panels, much welcomed by the teachers. This cooperation at regional level was innovative, its results reflected a fair consensus between teachers and authorities and were fully acceptable in the schools. By contrast, national discussions on proposed changes in examination arrangements in most cases either failed to achieve agreement between the interests concerned or failed to convince successive Secretaries of State to approve radical changes. Is there a moral here for curriculum change as well, which the current Secretary might do well to consider?

The problems at national level were nowhere better illustrated than in the attempt to broaden the sixth-form curriculum, with which the Council was charged at its first meeting. Working Paper No. 5, 1966, began by saying:

> There are two main reasons why the time is ripe for discussion of sixth form work and some reformulation of its pattern. First, sixth forms have expanded rapidly in recent years and contain many pupils whose needs may best be met by some alternative to 'A' level courses and the conventional '3 "A" level' curriculum. Secondly, measures are needed to counteract excessive specialization, which has been the object of so much criticism, and to lend support to the efforts made by individual schools to broaden the curricula of their pupils, whether they are proceeding to higher education or not.[7]

The paper made proposals for major and minor studies, together with general studies. Discussions took place with member interests and with the Standing Conference on University Entrance (SCUE). As a result, new proposals were made in Working Paper 16, which included a commentary by SCUE. Sir Robert Aitken, the Chairman of SCUE, set out in a letter to the Chairman of the Schools Council:

> ... what appeared to the Standing Conference to be the area of agreement between themselves and the Schools Council:
> (a) that the prospective increase in size and academic range of sixth form populations makes curricular reform necessary to meet the various needs of sixth formers.
> (b) that it is desirable to reduce specialisation and broaden the scope of study in the sixth form.
> (c) that it is desirable that a pupil's choice of subjects, for

study in the sixth form and the university, in so far as it narrows his career opportunities, should be made as late as possible in his school career.

(d) these aims are likely to be achieved only if the curriculum is planned on a 'modular' basis, ie, in terms of major subjects studied each for so many periods and minor subjects studied each for half that number of periods, from which various groups may be chosen.[8]

The paper revealed two things of particular relevance to my present contribution: the difficulty of getting adequate statistics from the DES who persisted in basing all their data on pupils' ages in January, so cutting across school-year groups; and the major contribution made by the ILEA whose studies of the changing sixth-form were extensively quoted in the Working Paper. There followed in 1968 the setting up of a joint Schools Council/SCUE working party, of which I was a member, and the Second Sixth-form Working Party of the Schools Council, of which I became Chairman.

It took literally years to get the DES to produce statistics actually recording the number of pupils in the sixth-forms by September ages and thus school-year groups. I recall long arguments with the DES statisticians before we succeeded in getting these vital data.

The two working parties produced a joint statement in December 1969, the Q and F proposals, which were rejected by the Council in 1970. The two working parties continued their work, rather more separately, the outcomes being papers by the Second Sixth-form Working Party, No. 45[9] and No. 46[10] alongside the Joint Working Party's Working Paper No. 47.[11] Paper No. 46 proposed a single subject examination for the 'new sixth-formers', the Certificate of Extended Education and at 18+ a single-subject examination:

(a) to support a normal programme of five equal subjects studied for two years beyond the present O-level standard, and

(b) to permit more extensive study in one or two subjects selected from these five.

The 18+ examination should therefore be available at two levels — the Normal level and the Further level, the results in both being expressed in terms of grades.[12]

Discussions of N and F went on and on. Almost everyone paid lip-service to broadening the curriculum but many, not least among the university academics, produced arguments why the particular proposals would not do. I got tired of it in the end and wrote an article in *The Times Educational Supplement* an open letter to the Chairman of the Council, Sir Lincoln Ralphs, which seems to me, ten years later, still to be worth reproducing.[13] (see appendix)

As the reader will be only too well aware, Sir Lincoln not only did not succeed, I have no reason to believe he really tried, and 'A' level is still with us. It was in my judgment a major failure of the Schools Council, perhaps a failure inevitable within the distributed structure of educational administration in this country.

In the consideration which I have tried to give in this chapter to the LEAs' role in the life and death of the Schools Council, I turn finally to what I believe to be the heart of the matter: how is curriculum change really brought about? It is clear from what has been said about the birth of the Council that at that time the LEAs believed that their responsibility for the curriculum was best carried out by leaving it to the teachers in the schools (not, be it noted the schools themselves in the sense of pupils, teachers, governors, parents) even though in some large authorities, such as the LCC/ILEA, the influence of the Inspectorate was considerable. This LEA stance of the early sixties no longer holds and many LEAs are now well and truly in the business of curriculum development, through in-service training, the issue of guidelines, in a few cases the issue of what are virtually instructions to schools. Moreover, governing bodies now in law have considerable responsibility for the curriculum, even though in most cases this still means very little infringement of teachers' autonomy. This radical change in the method of development of, influence over and in a few cases, effective control of the curriculum has taken place within the lifetime of the Schools Council and in my judgment for two reasons: first, the enormous stimulus which the very existence and work of the Council itself gave and second, the difficulties, of which the Council became aware, of effectively disseminating Schools Council projects, of 'selling' the product to a conservative and independent-minded profession.

There is no doubt that the Schools Council has been the major agent in stimulating, encouraging and providing ideas for curriculum development, though alongside it other bodies such as Nuffield and the subject associations have also been active. It was the Schools Council which put curriculum change on the map, which involved thousands of teachers directly in it and which established a climate of opinion in which development became an expected norm. How was it that after twenty years, no great pleas for stay of execution came from either the teachers or the LEAs? The answer lies, in my view, in my second factor, the problems of dissemination. It may be a centralist Secretary of State who decided to terminate the Council but he was able to do it because the LEAs had by now learned to exercise a considerable influence on the curriculum and had established at the level of the individual authority a situation of cooperation with 'their' teachers far more effective than had been or ever could be established at national level.

Professor Wrigley, to whose paper I have already referred, describes the problem better than I can do. In the sixties and early seventies, he says:

> We were very confident. We thought that we would avoid in England the mistakes made in other parts of the world, particularly in the United States where the failure of large scale curriculum development became evident at an early stage. We felt that by keeping our feet on the ground, by organizing feedback, by using formative evaluation, by making sure that the work was done throughout the country in various local institutions that we should avoid the airy fairy nature of certain kinds of innovation. We were slow to see the abiding difficulty of effective innovation. We felt that by having teacher control of the Schools Council committees we had solved the question of participation. This is, of course, not so. A teacher is likely to be more sympathetic to an innovation if he or she participates himself. So the question of the dissemination and implementation of the large curriculum development projects was recognized rather slowly and even when the problems were recognized the solutions have proved to be very difficult. It has become clear that before innovations will be accepted in practice in the schools, the teachers concerned will need to be involved, will need to have the support of their colleagues, and will need to feel that they have adequate resources. The research and development movement took some time before it became the research development and dissemination movement.[14]

What were the LEAs doing alongside the work of the Schools Council? I have already described the influence of the ILEA inspectorate in London and in some of the big authorities. More widespread was the steady growth of in-service training within the individual authority and particularly important in this was the growth of teachers' centres. In 1964, the existence of a single teachers' centre was a matter of remark. Birmingham was the pioneer, the LCC followed. In 1984 an authority without one would be remarkable, many have several and the ILEA has pretty well one for each curriculum subject. The work of the CSE examination boards, as I have described them earlier, contributed to these developments.

I would not wish to do less than justice to the Schools Council's own efforts to achieve effective dissemination of the work of projects. The appointment of field officers was a key development and these officers played a vital role in getting Schools Council projects known, a role which both stimulated and took advantage of the growth of teachers' centres and local in-service training. I recall that while, in the early days, project budgets included little or nothing for dissemination, in later years we would not approve a project which did not make such provision. But the whole thing seemed to become more and more long drawn-out and Project Technology seemed to go on for ever. (I cannot from direct experience speak of the later years of the Council). My general conclusion, however, would be that we, the LEAs, were right to agree to the setting up of the Schools Council, right to give it the participation and support which we did, right to put resources into it — never very great in comparison with the cost of schooling itself — and right to give its projects support. But I would say that in the process we learned that curriculum development belongs essentially at the local level, to the teachers, to their professional advisers and officers and, in the final analysis, to their employers.

Appendix

My dear Sir Lincoln ...
Eric Briault

My colleagues and I on the sixth-form working parties have set out all the arguments at length in well-considered prose, in our reports, and have given much time and thought to the issues. The time is approaching for decisions. So I have a mind to be rather less formal. Here goes.

I begin with 10 good reasons for accepting the second sixth-form working party package.
(a) CEE.

1. The new sixth-formers need a new sixth-form examination, CSE style, single subject; if each subject were planned on the basis of its being one of five main subjects studied, this would suit very nicely.

2. The new sixth-formers stay only one year, so it must be planned to meet a one-year course.

3. The one-year stayers don't have much in the way of O level equivalents, so the target group must centre on CSE average performers; but there is no reason why the top end shouldn't be well over O level.

4. The 17-year-old leavers want a result that employers can understand and further education can use, so one grade must equal CSE grade 1.

So let's settle the pattern, decide on the package of which it is a part and *get on with it*.
(b) N.

5. The sixth-form curriculum needs broadening (who said that and how many years ago?)

and therefore more subjects; four's too much like three and six is too many, so make it five.

6. Most 18-year-old leavers are not going to the university, so listen to the employers and the colleges who would like them to have had a broader education (might get more literate scientists and even some numerate linguists, too).

7. We need to make a fresh start on 18-plus examinations so plan five Ns as normal and hope the schools will use them wisely (anyone can defeat any examination system if they try hard enough).

8. CEE instead of CSE-O level repeats plus five Ns will cost less teaching time than the present arrangements. (ever met anything less economic than A level teaching in some schools at present?)

(c) F.

9. But after all, degree courses are important and some subjects at least are consecutive in their learning style, so let us send people up to the university ready to start; and we can't afford four-year first degrees;

10. And people do like some subjects better than others and develop intellectually by intensity of study, so give them a chance.

So again, let's settle the pattern, decide on the package and replace A level completely by 1978.

The rest of what may be worth saying at this stage might be addressed first to all the people who at the moment are telling Schools Council what to do or not to do, and second, if I dare be so bold, to the chairman of the Schools Council himself.

First, to the givers of advice and especially to those who will put their hands up or keep them down at a couple of critical meetings of the governing council of the Schools Council. Do you want any change or don't you? You were the people who told my colleagues and myself that your august body had firmly decided that the sixth-form curriculum should be broadened and you said the universities agreed. Did you really mean it? And if so have you the collective wisdom to back the best package you are likely to get, so that you can advise the Secretary of State unitedly? (If you are obviously split, guess who will decide what?) You do not imagine anyone is going to try again this decade, do you?

If you all turn up mandated, instructed to vote for nothing but the special version you put in your official observations, you will all cancel out and there will be nothing left but a quiet smile on the face of the A level tiger. Of course the tiger would not be reluctant to leave you with CEE and if you try and stretch it to cover the more able (but of course non-U) pupils and if you keep havering as to whether it is for a one-year course or a two-year course, there will not be any need for N will there? That is why you have got to look at the package and not rush madly after CEE by itself, regardless.

And so to the chairman, God bless him. My dear Sir Lincoln, this really is going to be a test of your chairmanship. I am not saying that the Schools Council stands or falls by a solution of the sixth-form curriculum and examinations issue. We all know the Schools Council has done, is doing, and will do a great deal more than that, much of it very valuable (though we sometimes feel we could do with a breather). But you will agree it is important. And so I do not envy you the task of securing a consensus.

But you really must take it on, my dear Lincoln, so as to show that the major body representing all parts of the education service can make (pace Mrs Thatcher) a major change. And not only to show that it can, but because it is right (if all we have said so far is true) that it should.

So it will not do, will it, to have a rigmarole of resolutions, amendments and counter-amendments at these critical meetings over which you will preside? You must persuade us to agree to what commands the greatest measure of agreement and what can reasonably be accepted by the universities, too. For yours will be the task after that of persuading the Secretary of State to agree. I for one have sufficient confidence in your powers of statesmanship to believe you can bring it off. And the best of British (or strictly speaking English and Welsh) luck!

Eric Briault is education officer of the ILEA and chairman of the Schools Council Sixth Form Working Party.

Notes

1 GOSDEN, P.H.J.H. (1973) 'The governance of the education system', *University of Leeds Review*, pp. 34–5.
2 MINISTRY OF EDUCATION, (1964) *Report of the Working Party on the Schools' Curricula and Examinations*, London, HMSO, p. 9.
3 AEC, A31a, note by Marjorie McIntosh, Brotherton Library, University of Leeds.
4 MINISTRY OF EDUCATION, (1964) *op. cit.* p. 9.
5 *Ibid.*, p. 13–14.
6 WRIGLEY, J. (1983) 'Confessions of a curriculum man', *Curriculum*, Vol. 4, No. 2, p. 35, and in this volume.
7 (1966) *Sixth-form Curriculum and Examinations*, School Council Working Paper No. 5, London, HMSO, p. iii.
8 (1967) *Some Further Proposals for Sixth-Form Work*, Schools Council Working Paper No. 16, London, HMSO, p. 1.
9 (1972) *16–19 growth and Response: 1 Curricular Bases*, Schools Council Working Paper No. 45, London, Evans/Methuen Educational.
10 (1973) *16–19 Growth and Response: 2 Examination Structure*, Schools Council Working Paper No. 46, London, Evans/Methuen Educational.
11 (1973) *Preparation for Degree Courses*, Schools Council Working Paper No. 47, London, Evans/Methuen Educational.
12 (1973) *16–19 Growth and Response: 2 Examination Structure*, Schools Council Working Paper No. 46, London, Evans/Methuen Educational, p. 12.
13 BRIAULT, E.W.H. (1974) My dear Sir Lincoln ..., The *Times Educational Supplement*, 15 February.
14 WRIGLEY, J. (1983) *op. cit.* p. 34.

The Middle Years

Geoffrey Cockerill

My memories of the Schools Council are contained almost entirely within a short period of eighteen months between late 1970 and mid-1972. The impressions are fragmentary but still vivid and affectionate. It was a vibrant place which provided unique experience for someone on loan from a local authority, school, university or in my case the DES. Teamwork by teachers, research workers, publishers and others was not only stimulating but essential if curriculum development by the Council was to attract support which it had no wish or power to command.

At that stage it seemed to have some hope of doing so. Mrs Thatcher, addressing the Governing Council in March 1973, said of the school leaving age: '... The decision to raise the age to sixteen was a government decision — taken in fact in the same year in which the Schools Council was set up, and it was the government which had to find the resources in terms of buildings and teachers to carry this decision into effect. But I feel bound to say that the heart of the operation was in the years of curricular preparation which it was the Council's own decision to undertake and with which it patiently persevered, even though the reform itself was temporarily postponed ... Teachers are in the thick of all these issues. If the Schools Council had not been brought to their aid in the 1960s, we should have had to set about creating a new body in the 1970s.'

What of the background? The 1970 White Paper showed that in 1971–72 expenditure on education in England and Wales would be £2.3 billion. No one could say accurately what was being spent at that time on curriculum development as a whole but a figure sometimes quoted was £2.5 million. If this broadly illustrative amount was even roughly correct the Council was consuming about a half of one thousandth of educational public spending, on examinations as well as curriculum work.

This being the level seen as affordable by national and local government (as paymaster partners), it was essential to use it wisely. To pick sensible routes between competing claims was a fundamental challenge. The Council's task was not to fill libraries with treatises but the more mundane and difficult one of helping teachers to serve their pupils, at all levels. If the pay-off was not in the schools it would be nowhere. The effectiveness of this impact on the schools became quite properly the debating ground among supporters and critics alike — and most people I met were a bit of both. Although curriculum development had existed as long as schools themselves, at a national level this was relatively untrodden territory apart from the work of the Nuffield Foundation which had helped to pave the way for the establishment of the Curriculum Study Group and hence of the Council itself; untrodden, that is, in terms of a specific remit, although it had been an implicit part of the work of HM Inspectors for well over a century.

One of the sensitive issues in my time, as I think at others, was the matter of teacher union representation. I recall a description, in the journal of a minority teacher organization, of the Council as 'the NUT's poodle'. I never saw it as this but the point was bound to be made because of the roughly *pro rata* allocation of places. I preferred the comments of Professor John Nisbet in his report on the Council for OECD in 1971:

> Three member interests hold a controlling power. The first two, the Department of Education and Science and the local education authorities, provide it with its finance. The third, the teachers, constitute a majority on its committees. To whom are the teacher representatives accountable? Their immediate accountability is to the union or association which nominates them. The teachers' associations, therefore — and in particular the National Union of Teachers, which has the largest number of members — have a special responsibility, in that they exert a powerful influence on the Council. To this extent, the health of the Schools Council is linked with the vitality of democracy in the teachers' associations.

It was (and is) absolutely vital to involve as many teachers as possible in curriculum development, whether nationally or locally inspired. Whether there could ever be ways of achieving this nationally without union support, I strongly doubt. Also, I feel it right to say that in the numerous working committees I attended my impression was of teachers coming together professionally rather than in a partisan spirit; if there were occasional hints of teacher politics this seemed understandable and acceptable. The worst aspect of the unions' majority voice lay I believe in the proprietorial image which this as a concept presented to the outside world, and which would hardly have been different whatever the particular form of democracy within any union. Prejudice can thrive on images. There may also have been a conservatism in the strategy of the Council stemming partly from union protectiveness but this can only be speculative.

In recalling impressions it is salutary to go back (it now seems a long journey) to the climate surrounding education at the start of the seventies. The sixties had been a high peak of education in public aspiration and political esteem. Major hopes (exaggerated in terms of quick returns) had been invested in the spread of comprehensive schools, the lengthening and enrichment of teacher education and the massive enlargement of higher education opportunity following Robbins. The leaving age was raised at last, after a final economic hiccup. The education service was seen by a great many as the engine which would reinforce and extend the good life by bringing to it the benefits of technology. And until the economy began to falter there was a broad political consensus about this way forward. Dissension about both comprehensive and public schools continued, yet there was a tacit acceptance that both were here to stay for the forseeable future. Overriding these issues and any other individual ones totally, however, was a general climate almost unreservedly pro-education. Mr Macmillan himself had addressed a meeting about the 1963 Year of Education, in Hamilton House. Sir Edward Boyle had accepted Robbins, applauded 'Half Our Future' and launched Plowden. The first Secretary of State for Education and Science (now Lord Hailsham) had set the seal on the foundation of the Council itself. Mr Crosland, picking up a similar baton, secured an increase in the output of teachers at the same time as maintaining the three year course. And as late as 1970 we had the 'Framework for Expansion'.

Yet education, even when it can be seen in retrospect as having been relatively non-party-political for a time (it is always political), is a ready hostage to public expectation of quick results almost as though it were a housebuilding programme. It is an easy scapegoat for economic or other malaise. If poor spelling or race prejudice or whatever cannot be cured immediately, why not?

The Council was bound to run up against this kind of problem. Even if the economic outlook had been brighter the timescale would have been against it. So far from producing results in the schools (which are anyway difficult to evaluate) in three or four years, it was doing well if published materials reached them in that period. Projects were in a Catch 22 situation. If materials came out quickly, had they been thoroughly worked on with teachers and then evaluated? If not, why was public money being wasted?

It was not only outsiders who expected more than could reasonably be delivered. There could be impatience within the Council, and sometimes rightly so, about the time taken. I have sometimes wondered whether public expectations were raised too high by the speeches and other publicity about the Council's work. Yet without this there would have been even less awareness among hard-pressed teachers of what it was all about. Despite the penetration of 'Dialogue' into all schools (and supposedly into all staff rooms), it was still common to meet teachers who knew nothing about the Council except its name.

Also in the early seventies the Council's budget was beginning to be scrutinized more critically by both central and local government. The honeymoon was almost over for anyone who regarded all money spent on curriculum development as being money automatically well spent. But any thunder was still a distant murmur. The Council was in its heyday. Teachers' Centres were springing up by the week. More Field Officers were being recruited (and what an asset they were) and a travelling exhibition was permanently on the road. The Anglo-American Primary Education Project was but one manifestation of the great interest overseas in the Council and in British education. The keynotes were still enthusiasm and optimism.

Yet questions were beginning to be asked, some justifiable, others less so, both within the Council and outside. For example, wide publicity for the fact that the Council had over a hundred projects in train in 1971, at a total cost of between £4m and £5m (much more in today's currency) was in danger of rebounding. How much had been published? Of this, how much had been bought by schools? How many schools had been involved in the preparation? Were there any ascertainable results? Among those with more patience, prepared to wait for the germination necessary in education, there tended to be a different kind of question. How many of the projects funded, and of those in train for funding, had resulted from a strategy deliberately thought out by the Council, and how many were the result of hopeful bids by people seeking support for their ideas and work? A typical reply within the Council was likely to be that the two coincided; that the Council's strategy was to be seen in its choice of proposals; and that in any case bids often resulted from prompting by staff in knowledge of what the Council was seeking. It remained the case that although some significant projects were commissioned from the outset, and even in effect put out to tender, others simply happened — subject of course to the relevant committee approvals.

Although this was defensible and just about acceptable, it seemed to fall short of the level of strategic input to be hoped for from a body charged with national curriculum development. There was some project work 'across the curriculum' which tried to bring a strategic view to bear, but the Council as a body did not give the impression (to me at any rate) of being geared up to evaluate seriously such work and to make its dispositions accordingly. The energetic and sometimes inspired commissioning of advice and materials for teachers was no substitute for consideration and decisions (in short, planning) as to ways in which the best available ideas and practices could be implanted securely in the schools, in co-operation (in my view only perhaps) with HM Inspectors and their local authority counterparts. There needed to be more systematic analysis of priorities and less reliance on the faith that a scatter of good seed would take root.

Even at more mundane levels the Council tended to avert its gaze from the business side of educational life. For example, concerns were beginning to be expressed, not least by some experienced members, about the cost of materials published by the Council; ie whether the purchase of a reasonably wide range would be possible within the capitation grants of many schools, even if they limited themselves only to the Council's output. There were other members and staff who regarded questions like this as little more than an irritant and suspected the motives. Yet it was arguable that the Council's value and future could have as much to do with matters of this kind as with faith in a philosophy.

I remember Harry Rée meeting some of us at the Council with the heartfelt plea . . . 'for goodness sake put more resources into dissemination, if necessary at the expense of new projects'. I have since seen that similar things were said later in evidence to Mrs Trenaman. There no doubt continued to be a tussle between the innovators and the consolidators, but there could have been a balance rather than a polarization.

If the Council seemed somewhat deficient in strategy about what it was trying to achieve, through what decisive means, in the curriculum, this was less true in the examinations area, where there were existing coherent systems against which ideas for change could be to some extent weighed. Examinations presented a target at which aim could be taken and for which people other than teachers, and ultimately the Secretary of State, were answerable.

Nobody, however, within the Council's terms of reference (drawn at this point directly from the Lockwood Report) was responsible for the curriculum apart from the individual school: 'each school should have its own curriculum and teaching methods based on the needs of its own pupils and evolved by its own staff'. As the Council never sought to amend this, it must be assumed to have been content not only to disclaim for itself any views about the content of the curriculum which could be held sufficiently strongly to be urged upon schools, but also in a sense to deny that the curriculum was in any way public property outside the school. I have observed that people within and outside education tend to be uneasy in varying degrees about this doctrine. They want schools to be autonomous provided they do sensible things! The constant reiteration of the doctrine in Council circles and publications could be interpreted perversely, and it sometimes was, as placing the autonomy of the teacher above what parents and others might see as being the needs of the child. I think it might have been possible to tilt the balance of attitudes a little without getting remotely involved in a centrally imposed curriculum.

I certainly believe that the Council's wish not to lay claim even to the mildest degree of authoritative curricular wisdom — to do with content or balance or teaching method — helped to make it an obvious target (perhaps an honourable thing to be) for those who believed there to be static knowledge and skills which it was the schools' job to purvey and from which all children could profit if only teachers and the education service generally would pull up their socks. Yet, however right the Council was in resisting naive attack, it could not afford to be cavalier about the unease which a lot of people felt. Whether they were right or wrong to feel it is irrelevant. A public body ignores public concern at its peril.

Without bowing to the grosser simplicities about standards of performance and its improvement, the Council might have been prudent to acknowledge (and here I stick out my neck) that there could be levels of formal attainment in schools which those outside might reasonably expect of young people at various stages; and have gone on to say that although it believed this was by and large already being achieved, it was an area in which evidence would be welcomed and in which the Council would take whatever action it could. Any other attitude was likely to be interpreted as a shrugging off of responsibility and to wrong-foot the Council in popular political terms. The man in the Mini may have been uncomprehending about new approaches to teaching but he might be excused for thinking that a body charged at his expense with responsibility for curriculum development should be responsive to any gut concerns about his children. A lot more could have been done to reassure ordinary people. There was too much emphasis in the Council on the needs of teachers, too little on public relations outside the profession. We explained what we were about to MPs from each of the main parties, and held conferences with local authority elected members as well as their officers; it was not enough.

I was never sure whether the resistance in the Council's blood-stream to considering what advice if any might be offered to schools on levels of pupil performance at which they might aim (making their own allowances for social and other difficulties), sprang from a conviction that this would be improper within the terms of reference, which I doubt; or that it was quite impossible for such advice to be constructed even by a teacher controlled body; or that it would be pedagogically harmful; or that teachers should never be subjected to authoritative guidance from outside. In personal discussion (the matter never in my recollection being ventilated in committee while I was there) the different objections tended to be fused. Whatever the reason, the Council's antennae seemed not to register adequately a genuine popular concern, at a time when school reorganization had left many parents and employers insecure in their expectations. If advice about standards was an unrealistic aim, the Council was very well placed to explore the matter thoroughly and to explain why. Either way, the Council showed a lack of strategic sense for which I must take my share of responsibility. As a footnote to these thoughts, I do not recall that there was ever any research into the likely attitudes of teachers as to guidance on standards which might be offered by the Council. If the question had arisen, in whatever form, the influence of the unions could have been crucial to the outcome.

I sense that the reluctance of members and staff (for the most part) to think in terms of performance stemmed only in part from a conviction that the schools would do better without it. There was in the background a folk memory of 'payment by results' and of the 'Hand-book of Suggestions'. The former role of HMI Inspectors seemed still to threaten. Making allowance for this, it was nevertheless strange to me that professionalism for teachers and autonomy for schools appeared to be thought sustainable only at the cost of regarding the contribution of HMI — who spend their lives in and around different schools, as hardly anyone else does — as having no more significance than that of every other contributor to the work. I would have liked to see a much closer relationship (and if possible some kind of partnership, though no one else is likely to agree) between the Council and the national and local inspectorates and advisory services, preferably against the background of a better developed strategy — although I think this might have followed. Such a concept might for all I know have been condemned on both sides. To readjust part of the role of HMI in this way could have been difficult in view of their special place, but not I suggest impossible. The necessary give and take on all sides would have been profound. But much of value might have come from such a powerhouse.

To retreat from speculation, it is uncontroversial to comment that the curricular autonomy of the schools as basic to Schools Council philosophy was the feature most remarked upon by the abundance of overseas visitors who came to find out more about this educational prophet which seemed to lack full honour in its own country. I remember some of us lunching a former Premier of France, who went away looking puzzled.

The only certainty about the Council is that its efforts were never fully appreciated. Even more conventional educational bodies can rarely satisfy evangelists or entirely confound doomwatchers. To take a trivial example, but one which illustrates in microcosm what the Council was to face more seriously on other fronts, there was the time when the schools had finally gone metric, after prodigious efforts by the Council and DES (there are areas in which partnership and some degree of prescription can work). I was telephoned by an irate tycoon to complain that his recruits could no longer work in feet and inches. What did the education service think it was doing?

I was fortunate to know the Council at perhaps its zenith. To serve it was a constant stimulus and challenge. I had, and still have, nothing but admiration for all those, teachers and others, who gave time and effort to it well beyong the reasonable calls of duty — in particular the Chairmen of the Council and its various committees. To some outside it must have seemed an uncomfortable intrusion. How could such a body deny the proper role of examinations as being to separate sheep from goats? If failure was not built in, what incentives could there be for the bright? Yet when O Level certification was eventually extended through the Council's efforts to grades below the previous pass mark there was hardly a murmur. If examinations designed to provide profiles of performance, and curricula seen as antecedent to examinations, are now becoming respectable policy aims, the Council undoubtedly contributed a large part of the yeast. It will be shown to have done so in other ways too, once public education feels some sunlight on it again.

The Welsh Dimension

Alan Evans

The odd thing about governments both in this country and
elsewhere is that they list buildings of historic or architectural
interest; they declare reserves for creatures and plants that are in
danger of extinction; they create National Parks to preserve
countryside of outstanding beauty; they cause preservation
orders to be put on trees; they buy works of art for their people;
they subsidize theatre and ballet; they commission music and
feed poets and writers; but the sound of 'minority' language is
anathema to them. Yet a language is more subtle and significant
than the most outstanding building, more fleeting than the rarest
of creatures and plants — desert rats knew the gutters of
Carthage and willows grew in the waters of Babylon. A
language is the most magnificent and awe-inspiring creation of
any people. No art can compare with its beauties and no science
can match the complexity of its structures. Yet who protects a
language when it is a minority language? How can anyone claim
to care deeply for any language and not care for all languages?
Show me a man who despises any language and I'll show you a
Philistine unworthy even of his mother tongue. The real pressure in Wales has come from those who are worthy of their
mother tongue and despise no language. As much as any it has
come from parents who have lost their Welsh and are anxious
that their children should find it. They know, these parents, that
if their children are to enter into their inheritance, the role of the
schools is vital for the language. And the role of the Schools
Council is vital for the schools.[1]

These words of Gwyn Jones, a former Chairman of the Committee for
Wales, state in eloquent terms the reason for its existence. For over a

quarter of a century the most significant fact in the schools of Wales has been a growing awareness of the place of the Welsh language within the curriculum. The work of the Schools Council in Wales has been a response to that awareness.

At its inception the Committee for Wales was given two functions: to exercise in relation to Wales the functions of the three curriculum steering committees,[2] including co-ordination of work in the different age ranges; and to advise the Governing Council and its other committees on the special needs and problems of schools and pupils in Wales, including examinations conducted in the Welsh language.

The Committee was composed of some twenty-seven members (including five co-opted members) drawn from the teacher associations, the Welsh Office, the Welsh Joint Education Committee (WJEC), the Trades Union Congress (TUC), the Confederation of British Industries (CBI), and the National Confederation of Parent Teacher Associations. The founding fathers of the Schools Council must have had considerable foresight in drafting this section of the constitution as they brought into being a parliament for education in Wales. This unique forum included the Chief Inspector, the Under Secretary at the Welsh Office, the Secretary of the WJEC, leading figures of the teaching profession in Wales, representatives from the Chief Education Officers, Advisers, Teacher Centre Wardens and the University of Wales, and proved over the years to be ideal as a deliberative body representing all sections of educational life in Wales. The Committee had the authority and the expertise to act as a committee of scrutiny in the field of curriculum development and examinations, as well as the confidence and the imagination to promote and administer major curriculum and assessment projects and programmes in the two languages of Wales, and in other areas of the curriculum and school organization that had particular significance for the schools of Wales. The Committee was fortunate in its choice of Chairmen and Secretaries; all the Secretaries, apart from the last, were seconded for three year periods from Her Majesty's Inspectorate in Wales. They provided skilful leadership and support in the many delicate and sensitive issues that formed the core of the work of the Committee. Factional or sectional politics hardly ever impeded this work, and on nearly all major issues there was a consensus on the priority to be allocated and the mode of operation to be followed. But despite this consensus, the critical faculties of individual members were not constrained, either by the dynamic of the Committee and its sub-committees, or by the area of Welsh educational life from which they were drawn.

In considering the remit to promote the Welsh language, social factors, particularly those arising from the home, could not be ignored for they were an important influence in shaping a child's grasp of language and in giving a new impetus to the teaching of Welsh. Although education alone would not be able to counter the apathy of society and the influences which bore on the use of Welsh, schools by being aware of the need for a concerted attack might be able to show society what should be supported in their work. In this sensitive situation the task of the Committee for Wales was two-fold: to promote the use of the language by its curriculum development work and to prepare a climate of opinion for the reception of this emphasis on the teaching of the language. The uniqueness of the problems of a bilingual society, and the choice which schools in such a society had to make, were recognized from the beginning. In its publication, *Y Gymraeg: Wynebu'r Dyfodol — Welsh: A Programme of Research and Development*[3], that choice was articulated in a series of questions:

Are they to retain and strengthen bilingualism?
If so, will this serve to enrich the thought and feeling to which pupils have access?
Are there values relevant to education in the added perspective and in the access which a second language gives to a second culture?
Do we know enough about the values of education of a two-culture society?

The recommendations contained in the document provided the basis for the Committee's Welsh language work. Its response was aimed at every level and type of schooling. The identification of problems and the establishing of priorities in a bilingual society are necessarily complex and in every decision it was necessary to measure with great sensitivity the diverse needs of monoglot children to ensure that no group suffered any learning impediment because resources for curriculum development in Wales were maldistributed. That major steps were taken in the improvement of Welsh language teaching for first language children and second language children without major recriminations from the majority of the population is a mark of the sensitivity with which the work was pursued and also of the general goodwill towards the aspirations of people in fostering the language.

Major projects were supported on the place of Welsh as a first language in the education of children at the primary stage and at the secondary stage. The project at the primary stage [4] aimed to develop teaching approaches to help children discover and use the varying language patterns they need in different situations. The material consisting of units for each term in a primary school was graded to reflect the development of children's reading abilities. The need to explore the variety of learning situations in the teaching of Welsh as a first language at secondary level and to look at the development of linguistic resources for Welsh speaking children formed the basis of the project at the secondary stage.[5] By setting up situations which provided pupils with a wide experience of language and its use it aimed to increase children's linguistic competence. The source books produced on a variety of themes illustrating the use of language were intended to promote the child's ability to respond to express himself or herself, and to foster an appreciation of literature.

The Committee was responsible for the development of the first reading scheme ever to be based on the structures of the Welsh language and firmly based on the language used by children and located in environments they were able to recognize[6]. The project was an attempt to overcome one of the major difficulties in teaching children to read. Many English schemes were alien and alienating for so many children. Teachers from thirty schools, mostly situated in Welsh-speaking areas, compiled extensive lists of children's spoken and written language. The frequency of the usage of the words was analyzed by a computer. Reading materials were based on the language patterns found and these reflected the children's interests which had been revealed during conversations with them in the project schools.

One of the problems of a culture increasingly dominated by another is that the language of the 'minority' culture tends to be restricted to the private domain and to those areas of experience which have moulded the culture. Welsh is exceedingly rich in literary, historical and theological expressions but the language of the 'majority' culture has become the vehicle for new knowledge. Therefore, until recently the Welsh language has not been greatly influenced by mathematical and scientific developments. The Committee for Wales recognized that if children were to be taught science and mathematics through the medium of their mother tongue suitable materials had to be prepared. A project[7] was mounted to provide text books in Welsh to increase the facility of both teachers and children in using the language. The importance of resource materials in the teaching of subjects through the medium of Welsh was recognized by the Committee in its publication of discussion papers and in its holding of conferences to discuss their relevance in such subjects as classics and modern languages.

The largest outlay of expenditure on the part of the Council for work in Wales involved the bilingual projects initiated by the Committee for Wales. The expenditure on the primary schools' project and that of the secondary schools represented the commitment of the Council to the bilingual culture of Wales and to the need to see bilingualism as the cohesive force in Welsh life. The primary schools' project[8] was set up to help children who spoke only English at home to understand and speak basic Welsh by the end of their primary schooling. A programme in which Welsh and English were used as the medium of instruction enabled children to learn a second language simultaneously with broadening their knowledge in other subjects. As soon as children had become familiar with hearing and speaking Welsh, half the day would be devoted to activities using this as the teaching medium and half to using English as the medium.

The difficulties of teaching Welsh as a second language in secondary schools have resulted from the different degrees of proficiency and the different levels of ability which pupils in the same group might display. The project on bilingual education in secondary schools[9] recognized those difficulties and the materials produced were written in three language categories reflecting the levels of difficulty. The use of the second language was seen as a tool of communication rather than an end in itself. Therefore the project aimed to introduce the communicative method of teaching language to teachers involved in teaching Welsh as a second language.

If Welsh is to be vital in the education of children in Wales it has to be seen to be part of the educational experience of every child. The Committee for Wales indicated its acceptance of this principle in the establishment of a project to provide Welsh medium diagnostic tests and remedial teaching materials.[10] Its aim was to survey the problems facing children with learning difficulties and facing teachers in schools using Welsh as the teaching medium, and in the light of the identified needs to develop appropriate teaching materials.

The Welsh language work of the Schools Council has been one of its greatest successes. One of the reasons for this has been that projects sponsored by the Committee for Wales have been a response to articulated needs. Another very potent element in the success has been the close liaison work with and the involvement of teachers in all levels of the work. This has gone far beyond practising teachers on monitoring bodies and has involved the professional expertise of teachers in their everyday work. The work on diagnostic tests and remedial teaching materials illustrated this approach. The work proceeded in three stages, the first of which was a detailed survey of needs in the particular field. By means of a questionnaire schools were requested to identify their needs. The priority of both primary and secondary schools was for a series of reading books. Primary school teachers also indicated the need for a pre-reading scheme, while teachers in secondary schools requested supplementary reading books. Having established these priorities, teachers were asked to suggest themes for reading schemes for children with learning difficulties. The second and third phases of the project have been concerned with the preparation of materials and diagnostic tests in accordance with the teachers' responses.

Welsh language work necessarily figured largely in the concern of the Committee for Wales but it never lost sight of the fact that the nation's bilingual culture might be manifested in other ways and that Welsh consciousness might be seen in the increasing interest in Welsh history. Its publications, projects and conferences therefore included other aspects relevant to education for a bilingual community, including Welsh studies in primary schools[11] and at sixth form level[12].

The Schools Council came into existence at a time when the role of the Welsh language in the education of children in Wales was undergoing change. Bilingualism had been accepted as a desirable goal for pupils educated in Wales and there was widespread agreement on its advantages for children in a society in which two languages were spoken. For the whole period of its being the Committee for Wales made a contribution to the renaissance of the Welsh language in education and saw its function, as promoting bilingualism and the particular culture which arises from two languages. Bilingualism implies a parity of worth between the two languages. The work of the Schools Council in Wales was in answer to the perceived needs of those who were concerned with the survival of the Welsh language in education. It attempted that work not by handing down its prescriptions from some Olympian height but by associating teachers at every level in its work.

The achievements of the Committee for Wales do not, however, rest solely on its language work: its pioneering endeavours in profile reporting, defining, delineating and combating disadvantage and disaffection, careers education and guidance, the curriculum and the organization of small rural primary schools are just a selection of the significant activities of the Schools Council in Wales in recent years. (A more detailed account of the stewardship of the Committee for Wales from 1978 to 1983 is set out as an appendix). This work led to the publication of the report by Frank Loosmore *Curriculum and Assessment in Wales*[13] (1979), the report by Jennifer Jones *Profile Reporting in Wales*[14] and two reports prepared by the Secretary, Mr Bernard Jones, on *Careers Education and Guidance in Wales*[15] and *Small Schools in Concert*[16].

These reports led in turn to day and residential disseminating conferences attended by local authority elected members, administrators and advisers of local education authorities, Her Majesty's Inspectors, teachers, academics, industrialists, trade unionists, parents, and representatives of the WJEC, the University of Wales and the Welsh Office.

The Loosmore Report, for instance, led to a piece of action research which involved schools in local authorities throughout Wales in re-examining their curricular provision in order to provide more effective learning strategies for all their pupils and particularly for those appearing to underachieve. The Jennifer Jones feasibility study involved four trial profile models being piloted in fifteen volunteer schools in several local authorities in Wales and led to the production of a model national profile in Wales. The high quality of this work and its interesting findings have been much commented upon in educational circles throughout England and Wales and the Welsh Joint Education Committee has now taken the national profile under its umbrella for further development and application at an all-Wales level. The small rural schools project also resulted in the organization of a national conference in order to disseminate its findings and to share the experiences of participating schools with other schools in England and Wales.

Such innovative work, commanding a judicious blend of political muscle and professional expertise has, on several occasions, given the educational system in Wales the opportunity to grapple with curriculum, assessment and school administrative problems that proved to be more recalcitrant within the administrative and political framework of the Schools Council in England. Those with experience of both the English and Welsh administrative systems consider that this difference is not solely a matter of size but is inextricably related to a common belief in the aims and objectives of the educational system in the bilingual culture of Wales. Whatever the explanation, the Committee for Wales was delighted when the Trenaman Report[17] (1981) commended the achievements of the Committee and endorsed its special position within the Schools Council.

In view of the recommendations of the Trenaman Report, the decision of the Secretary of State for Education and Science and the Secretary of State of Wales in April 1982 to abolish the Council, including the Committee for Wales, was met with surprise and incredulity. Much had been achieved in curriculum development and assessment in Wales over the three decades of the Committee's existence. That these achievements should be set aside by a Secretary of State with scant regard for the contribution of the teaching profession and its representatives was reminiscent of an Orwellian world where the Ministry of Truth proclaimed:

War is peace
Freedom is Slavery
Ignorance is Strength

Is it not reasonable to believe that the education service in Wales deserved better?

Appendix

Work Undertaken by the Schools Council Committee for Wales since 1978

1 Teaching of Reading in Welsh Project — one year after-care service to this project which produced the first reading scheme in the Welsh Language. Preparation of video-tapes for in-service use.
2 Bilingual Secondary Education Project — one-year after-care service to this project designed to produce materials and develop new teaching approaches for children learning Welsh but with above average proficiency in Welsh on entering secondary school.
3 Welsh as a First Language at the Primary Level — one-year after-care service to this project designed to produce materials for Welsh First Language pupils; preparation of in-service video tapes.
4 Welsh Medium Diagnostic Tests project — a major project to produce diagnostic tests in Welsh Language and supplementary remedial teaching materials.
5 National Conference 'Two Languages for Life'.
6 'Teaching of Modern and Classical Languages through the medium of Welsh' — national conference and working party to produce materials.
7 Working Party producing materials in Welsh for use in school worship (primary and secondary levels).
8 Exploratory Study on Curriculum and Assessment in Wales — one year study — report published 1981. Programme of follow up work being undertaken — further report published September 1983. Collaboration with Welsh Consumer Council on the issue of Home-School links.
9 Profile Reporting in Wales — national conference and two-year feasibility study/development work. Working parties established in mathematics, craft and personal qualities/social skills — report published November 1983.
10 Joint BBC (Wales)/Committee for Wales Working Party developing material and radio broadcasts for schools on teaching of Welsh History.
11 LCD project (Dyfed) — development of local materials related to history/geography/social sciences project.
12 LCD project (Gwynedd) — development of 'O'/CSE Mode III course in technology.
13 Support for Powys LCD project on 'visual literacy' (media studies).
14 National in-service course on review of mathematics curriculum followed by establishment of twelve dissemination centres/workshop groups — follow-up work.

15 Curriculum and Organisation in Primary Schools in Wales. Support for four Welsh local education authorities exploring aspects of this problem within specified rationale — national conference March 1983.
16 Support for Powys LCD project — nursery education in primary schools.
17 Disaffection in Welsh Secondary Schools — national conference December 1982.
18 Curricular Links in Science between Primary and Secondary Schools — work being sponsored in seven authorities.
19 Careers Education — conferences convened in each LEA in Wales — follow-up work under consideration.
20 LCD project (Clwyd and Gwynedd) — science for children with special needs.
21 Support for Gwynedd LCD project — problems of mixed ability teaching.
22 The Teaching of Mathematics (Cockcroft) — proposed follow-up work.
23 Conference in March 1982 — Bilingual Secondary Level Project — workshop groups engaged in follow-up work.
24 Support for Music Dissemination Centre in Swansea.
25 Support for Statistical Education Dissemination Centre in Gwent.
26 Exploratory Study on Nursery Education in Primary Schools — support of one-year study by Powys LEA.

Conference reports

Exploratory Study on Curriculum and Assessment in Wales: research report and summary report
Curriculum Reappraisal: experiences of groups of schools engaged in re-examining their curricular provision
Two Languages for Life
Profile Reporting in Wales
Bilingual education in the Secondary Schools of Wales
Disaffection in Secondary Schools in Wales
Careers Education and Guidance in Wales
Small Schools in Concert: report of conference on the small rural primary school

Miscellaneous Publications

Welsh Studies in the Primary School: a working party report
Reading in the Middle Years of Schooling: Occasional paper from the Humanities Committee
Molecules and Matter: an occasional paper for teachers of the WJEC 'A' Level physics syllabus from the Maths/Science Faculty Committee
Topics in Welsh History: a resource pack to accompany radio broadcasts
Framework of the School Curriculum/Welsh in the School Curriculum: response to the DES/WEO document
Teaching Modern Languages and Classics through the Medium of Welsh: an occasional paper from the Language Faculty Committee

Alan Evans

The Shortage of Physics Teachers: occasional paper from the Maths/Science Faculty Committee

Curriculum and Organisation of Primary Schools in Wales: The Small Rural School: progress report from the project

Profile Reporting in Wales: discussion paper following a two-year feasibility study

Planning for Progress: response to HMI discussion document

Committee for Wales Award booklet 1980–1982: summary of account of activities funded by Committee for Wales

Gyda'n gilydd: a book of material in Welsh for use in School Worship in Secondary School

Modern Languages and Classics through the Medium of Welsh: material in French studies, French language, German and Latin

Six editions of Wales Science Bulletin: now replaced by *Quest*

Five editions of bi-annual magazine *Quest* for all schools in Wales

Project material related to:—

(a)   Welsh as a First Language at Primary Level
(b)   Welsh as a First Language at Secondary Level
(c)   Teaching of Reading in Welsh
(d)   Bilingual Education 5–11: evaluation report
(e)   Bilingual Secondary Education

Information activities

Purchase of material from London-based projects which has been catalogued and made available for loan to schools, colleges and visitors to Information Centre.

Bi-annual major exhibition at Urdd and National Eisteddfodau and several smaller exhibitions mounted at centres and colleges throughout Wales. Permanent exhibition of project material at the Information Centre with a changing range of projects being diplayed.

Constant queries from teachers, students, etc, on general or specific Schools Council activities and material.

Committee for Wales Awards Scheme

Under this scheme, awards — normally ranging from £50 to £300 — are made to groups of local teachers to further their curriculum development activities. Since its inception in 1980, thirty-three grants have been awarded totalling £6,635.

Notes

1 National Union of Teachers (1979) *Secondary Education Journal*, Vol. 9, No. 1, March.
2 These functions were retained when the Schools Council adopted in 1978 a new constitution replacing Steering Committees A, B and C and Governing Council by its Finance and Priorities Committee, the Professional Committee and Convocation.
3 DES (1967) *Schools Council Welsh Committee*, HMSO.
4 Welsh as a First Language at the Primary Level (7–11), 1973–77.
5 Welsh as a First Language at the Secondary Stage (11–17), 1969–75.
6 Teaching of Reading in Welsh (4–8), 1974–77.
7 Science and Mathematics in Welsh Medium Schools (5–13), 1969–73.
8 Bilingual Education in Welsh Primary Schools (5–11), 1968–77.
9 Bilingual Education in Welsh Secondary Schools (11–14), 1974–77.
10 Welsh Medium Diagnostic Tests and Remedial Teaching Materials, 1981–83.
11 Welsh Studies in Primary School, 1979.
12 Sixth Form General Studies in Wales, 1973.
13 *Curriculum and Assessment in Wales: An Exploratory Study*: F.A. Loosmore, 1981.
14 *Profile Reporting in Wales*: report by J. Jones, 1983.
15 *Careers Education and Guidance in Wales*: report of a series of one-day seminars, 1981.
16 *Small Schools in Concert*: report of a conference on the small rural primary school, 1983.
17 *Review of the Schools Council*: report by N. Trenaman, DES, 1981.

[The author would like to acknowledge the valuable comments and criticisms of Mr Ken Donovan, the NUT's Education Officer in Wales, who has had a particular interest in bilingual policies and strategies in schools in Wales throughout the 1970s and 1980s].

The Review

Alex Smith

One of the most interesting features of the Schools Council was the simple fact that it existed. When one thinks about it, there is no such thing as an Industries Council, along to which teachers and others can go to comment upon and criticize what industries do. (An idea along such lines was raised by Sir Peter Parker in the Dimbleby lecture of 1983.)

There is not such thing as a Universities Council for Curriculum and Examinations along to which teachers and others can go to comment upon and criticize what universities do. In my view there is great need for such a Council, for there are aspects of university education which are positively harmful to our national well-being, for example the dislike shown by universities for the practical activities of designing and making.

There is no such thing as a Parents Council, along to which teachers and others can go to comment upon and criticise what parents do — and teachers could make many sharp comments on that subject. But there is, or at any rate there was, a Schools Council, along to which universities, parents, industrialists, trades unionists, churches, validating bodies could go — and wanted to go — to comment on the nature and content of education in our schools. That, in principle, was a marvellous meeting-ground, which ought to have been maintained and developed, and applied to other sectors such as the universities and industry. It was an imaginative concept full of potential, and with much vision, too much imagination and vision it would seem for the men of the Department of Education and Science. So they extinguished it.

It is true that the reality of the Schools Council fell short of the ideal, but that is probably true of all of our social institutions.

I became Chairman of the Schools Council in 1975, in succession to Sir Lincoln Ralphs. I had been invited to do so by Sir William Pile, who was then the Permanent Secretary at the Department of Education and

Science. My inclination had been to turn it down, for I was not familiar with the works of the Council, and it was clear that the Chairmanship would require a great deal of time and effort on top of that required in my role as Director of Manchester Polytechnic. However, I had long conversations with Sir William in which he gave me much of the background, and when he assured me that I would have the support and help of the Department, I agreed to take it on. I was convinced that Sir William wanted the Council to succeed. The Secretary of State at the time was Mr Reg Prentice, and my selection as Chairman had his full support.

Shortly after I had taken over the Chair, two things happened. Reg Prentice expressed some criticisms of trades unions. This, apparently, is an unwise thing for a Labour minister to do, and he became the target for much abuse. He was moved from the office of Secretary of State, and Mr Fred Mulley took over. Also, Sir William Pile was moved from the post of Permanent Secretary and Sir James Hamilton was appointed to succeed him.

The Yellow Paper

It seemed to me that these events marked, or coincided with, quite a change in attitude, the first manifestation of which was the infamous Yellow Paper. The Yellow Paper was supposed to be an internal document prepared by the Department of Education and Science for the Prime Minister, Mr Callaghan, but it was leaked to the press, which had something of a field-day with its contents. The paper was generous in its criticisms of others, but had no word, no hint, of self-criticism of the DES. It was critical of the schools and it was harsh in its criticisms of the Schools Council, describing its performance as mediocre.

The paper summarized criticisms that were fairly widely expressed about weaknesses in schools, and went on to assert that HM Inspectorate, 'the most powerful single agency to influence what goes on in schools, both in kind and standard', should have an increased role. It failed to ask the very obvious question of what the Inspectorate, if it was such a powerful agency, had been doing during the decades in which the deterioration had occurred. As an example of a well-reasoned case it was singularly unimpressive.

I was very taken aback. I doubt whether the performance of the Department of Education and Science over the years gives it much entitlement to refer to the performance of any other body as mediocre, but I had been assured of their support. If, I wondered, this is what they do when they support you, how do they behave when they dislike you? It was professional conduct of a kind that I was not accustomed to. The DES, after all, were members of the Schools Council. If the Council's performance in their judgment was mediocre, what efforts had they made as members to raise the standards of performance? What attempts had they made, as members, to express their criticisms within the Council? In my time I had seen none. By the conventional standards of professional conduct to which I had long been accustomed, I would have expected members of an organization to have the good manners and the good sense to express any criticisms they felt of the organization within the organization first, and to put some effort into putting things right. But the DES did not do so.

At the time I was so angered at the conduct of the DES that I felt I had to do something to dispel the mist through which they perceived the education service in general, and their role and that of HMI in it, and in particular to present a more balanced account of the role of the Schools Council, and so I wrote an open letter to the Prime Minister, which is reproduced as follows:

The Rt Hon James Callaghan, PC, MP
Prime Minister
10 Downing Street
London SW1   28th October, 1976

Dear Prime Minister,

It is with a mixture of dismay and anger that I have read through the report, 'School Education in England: Problems and Initiatives', which was sent to you in July by the Secretary of State for Education and Science, and which has been so widely publicized in the last few days.

I am not very disturbed by the suggestion therein that there is need for a core curriculum. I think that this has been badly reported and blown up into an unnecessary furore. I have no fears of discussions on this matter. What dismays me is the bias in the report.

It starts off with a brief summary of the concerns felt about primary and secondary schools, a summary that gives a very reasonable account of the criticisms and anxieties that are fairly widely felt about weaknesses in schools. The report then goes on a little later to state that 'HM Inspectorate is without doubt the most powerful single agency to influence what goes on in schools, both in kind and standard.... It is the oldest instrument for monitoring the education system and, from this primary function, it derives a second major role, that of improving the performance of the system.'

There are many in education who would not share that lack of doubt. However, were I the recipient of this report, my immediate reaction would be to ask what, if the weaknesses in schools summarized earlier in the report exist, this most powerful single agency, with a major commitment to improving the performance of the system, has been doing during the decade or two during which these weaknesses have been developing. The report shows that there is a clear need for a firm appraisal of the performance of HM Inspectorate, yet it contains not a word of criticism of it. On the contrary, it blandly suggests an increased role.

Neither does the report contain any word of self-appraisal of the Department of Education and Science. Instead, it throws criticism at others, at the teacher unions and at the Schools Council.

On the first of these, I can only express surprise as an individual that a member of your government should express such criticism, for my understanding is that it is your government's policy to involve trades unions fully in policy and decision-making. I would add that I am as concerned as anyone at the steady infiltration into our social institutions of people with political commitment to tear down the fabric of our society.

What does anger me, however, is the brash criticism of the Schools Council which is made in the report. I wish that, if the DES felt such criticisms, they had had the courage to express them directly to the Council, in the Council. They are after all members of the Council. However, they have made them directly to you, and I feel that I must try to present you with a much more balanced account.

Let me explain first that, when I was invited, a little over a year ago, by the Secretary of State for Education and Science to become Chairman of the Schools Council, I knew almost nothing about it. I am not a school teacher or headmaster or administrator of schools, and I have had virtually no involvement in schools. I was most reluctant therefore to take on the assignment, particularly since I have more than enough work to do in my job at Manchester. However, I was persuaded to try, my understanding being that the DES wanted a good Schools

Council — I certainly had no reason to expect then that the DES would undermine the Council by expressing adverse criticism in the way they have to you. I accepted the assignment with a feeling that, if I did not like it, if it did not like me, or if it was an impossible body to run, I could resign and get on with my work in Manchester.

My reluctance soon gave way to a profound enthusiasm. I find the Council a remarkable body. For all its inadequacies and short-comings (and like any human institution it has plenty), it is a partnership in education which is working. It may be creaking and there may be plenty of tensions within it, but it is working as a partnership, and that is a precious achievement in our society.

It is easy to criticize. Many people do, some of them very foolishly; I can, and do, criticize the Council, but I do so within the Council, and I am well aware of ears ready to hear and minds open to consider. It is not difficult to think of possible improvements to the organization or the structure or the constitution of the Council. What is much more important is the evolution of attitudes throughout the Council. I approach my role as Chairman with three consistent viewpoints.

(1)   as a parent; it is difficult to conceive of a representative parent but, being neither school teacher nor administrator, I try to assess issues from my standpoint as a parent;

(2)   as an employer; for a long time in my career I was a manager in industry, and I think I have some understanding of the viewpoints of employers, diverse though they may be;

(3)   as someone deeply interested in the relationship between education and the general state of social and economic well-being of our country.

It is this third issue that is now engaging your attention. I feel that the whole education service deserves some heavy criticism for the alienation that exists between education and the means whereby we as a nation earn our living. It is not an easy matter to change, and I am quite convinced it will not be changed by any form of coercion, by any pressurizing of young people to take particular courses. It will only be changed by changing attitudes, by making the involvement in the means whereby we earn our living attractive, and enabling young people to understand its significance. The purpose of education is to produce an educated and not a servile people, and I regard it as an essential fundamental characteristic of an educated nation that it should understand, support, and take pride in, the means whereby it earns its living. This is not achieved at present; to do so must be our aim, and there are no short cuts to it.

I see two main approaches in education to achieve this aim. One is to introduce into the schools the teaching about industrial society as part and parcel of our culture, just as we teach about our history and our literature. With the cooperation of the CBI and the TUC, the Schools Council is tackling this whole problem, and one of the most encouraging features of the venture is the enthusiastic involvement of the teacher members of the Schools Council.

The second approach that I would like to see is a correction to the imbalance in higher education that has been produced by an over-expansion of full-time study. It is not surprising to me that this causes an alienation, particularly in our most able young people, from the world of industrial work, and a preference for the academic or professional career. It is a built-in characteristic of the system. What we need to construct is a new pattern of education which is based upon a partnership between the world of education and the world of work, and that is something that calls out for a government strategy.

During this year, I have given a number of talks on this theme — the relationship between education and the nation's social and economic condition — to groups of educators throughout the country. I am astonished at the warmth of reception and understanding that the ideas receive. There is a great willingness to tackle this, the most profound challenge confronting education. This is the change in attitude that has been taking place in the last year or so, and particularly so in the Schools Council. Rather sadly, it seems not to have been noticed by the DES.

I am very glad indeed that you are asking questions about education. I feel that you were entitled to a fairer, more helpful, more thoughtful and more knowledgeable reply.

Yours sincerely,
ALEX SMITH

The Yellow Paper was real below-the-belt stuff. Whatever validity there may or may not have been in its criticisms, its colour was very appropriate.

Standards Rule, OK?

Another manifestation of the general hostility towards the Schools Council occurred in 1976 with all the rumpus over what became known as the Willmott Report. It was concerned with standards.

In the 1970s there was a rising tide of criticism and concern about standards. People are right to be concerned about standards in education, but I often felt then that the concern ought to spread to other aspects of our social life, to standards of housing, standards of parenthood, standards of workmanship and willingness to work, standards of respect for law and order, standards of journalism and so on. It is difficult to have schools with high standards in a not-very-high-standards society, and it is quite wrong to transfer to the schools a vague sense of guilt for what is happening in the rest of our social structure.

Criticism of schools is nothing new. It is a well-established English custom. In Scotland and Wales they tend to respect school education; in England we criticize it. I have met many teachers who unhesitatingly say that standards in education ought to be better. (How many journalists I wonder make a similar assertion about their profession?) But the question of whether or not standards are slipping is a very difficult one. The more we considered the question and studied the work that was in hand to throw some light on it, the more we realized what an immensely complex question it is, and its consideration is not helped by what happened to a report on the matter, commonly referred to as the Willmott Report.

To give it its full title it is 'CSE and GCE Grading Standards; the 1973 Comparability Study' by Alan S Willmott. It was commissioned by the Schools Council and carried out by the National Foundation for Educational Research, and it was meant to provide a baseline so that some assessment might be made of what effects might be caused by the raising of the school leaving age.

The report was heavily qualified with caveats about the validity of its assumptions. Nevertheless, the author expressed his belief that his results demonstrated a slight fall in subject grading standards in the period 1968–73. There was a hint, no more than that, of a decline in standards, interpretable as such if one accepted in full the validity of the author's assumptions, and the validity of his statistical methodology. The report was also open to interpretations which were less favourable.

Within the Council we were trying hard to understand the report, to understand the methodology used, to assess its findings in a thoughtful professional way, when all hell was let loose. The report fell into the hands of a Member of Parliament, Dr Keith Hampson, who handed it to the press, and from the very slender evidence in the report some very lurid headlines were concocted. For example, the Daily Mail of 3 July 1976 reported:

GCE survey shocks education chiefs

EXAMS—THE CRUMBLING STANDARDS

For those involved and responsible for standards in education, the Willmott Report was extremely unsatisfactory and open to a very great deal of criticism. For the Daily Mail, however, the caveats, the qualifications, the doubts and uncertainties were as nothing, and the meagre evidence and argument assembled by Dr Willmott was magnified out of all proportion. It was a disgraceful performance, which told one much more about the crumbling standards of integrity in journalism than it did about standards in examinations.

To make matters worse there were allegations by Dr Hampson that the Schools Council was trying to suppress and conceal the findings of the report:

MP claims cover-up on school standards

Far from it. The Schools Council had commissioned the report and was struggling to understand and to interpret it. It was an incident which reflected little credit either on Dr Hampson or on journalism.

The teachers' organizations, predictably, reacted rather strongly to the tirade of criticism in the press, which was a pity. The report, if anything, was not a criticism of teaching, but a criticism of the examining boards. One commentator (Robert Wood of the University of London, School Examinations Department) observed:

> Here is a report which contains two pages of caveats, any one of which, if true, would invalidate the results obtained... I do not think the results are sound at all... none of the figures which have been produced can be trusted... You do not need to publish suspect results (much less over-interpret them) in order to discuss methodology.

Interestingly enough, there was another draft report on standards circulating within the Schools Council at about the same time, entitled: 'Comparability of Standards at 'A' level as between 1963 and 1973' by Christie and Forrest. This report concluded that 'A' level standards had not fallen.

It was just as available for leaking to the press as the Willmott Report, but the Daily Mail ignored it, and Dr Hampson did not accuse the Council of concealing it. A favourable statement about exams, such as the Christie and Forrest report made, was one of no interest to them.

The incident did much to expose the extent of hostility felt amongst journalists towards the Schools Council, and throughout it all there was not a word of defence of either the Schools Council or the schools from the Department of Education and Science.

The 16+ Examination

Many years before I had become Chairman of the Schools Council work had been initiated on the concept of a single examination system in schools for children at the age of 16, to replace the dual system of the GCE 'O' levels and the CSE. When the dual system was introduced, it had been expected that there would be very little overlap between the two examinations, with very few children wanting to do both. In practice, a very considerable overlap had developed, and many children who had been advised to take the CSE were insisting on sitting the 'O' level as well. The case for a common system was becoming a strong one.

The proposal to develop such a system was formalized during the period of my chairmanship, and submitted to the Secretary of State in July 1977. In October I was invited by the Secretary of State, Mrs Shirley Williams, to be shown the draft of the response that had been prepared for her and which she was going to announce in the House of Commons on the following day. I was quite appalled at the general tone of hosility which permeated the response. Criticisms of the proposal were expressed in extremely pungent terms; it was hostile to the point of scurrility.

I appealed to Mrs Williams to tone down the hostility, and to her great credit she did. We spent some two hours or so modifying the more vitriolic phraseology in the draft until she had no more time to spare and had to leave to fulfil other commitments. The formal response which emerged on the following day was a much more reasoned, much less hostile, document. Even so, it was still pretty hostile, and the press had a time of it knocking the Schools Council. Inevitably I was left wondering why it was that people, of whose support I had been assured, were doing the drafting in terms of such damaging hostility. The proposal was shelved to allow time for the clarification of some of the issues.

I mention this because, as an observer now of the world of education rather than a participant, I found it very interesting that, some years later when Mr Mark Carlisle was the Secretary of State for Education and Science, he announced the intention to introduce a common examination system at 16. The phrases and the arguments used to justify the introduction were very much the same as the phrases and the arguments used by the Schools Council in 1976. I find it hard to escape the conclusion that in 1976 the DES gave more priority to undermining the Schools Council than to giving serious consideration to the proposal to alter the examination system.

Finance

The conduct and the content of education, the questions of what we teach, and why, and how, and at what stage, are amongst the most important questions in the whole tapestry of our nation's affairs. So profoundly important are decisions in education that they are really of far greater significance in the long run than choice of government. The effects of decisions in education, of their implementation or non-implementation, may not manifest themselves for decades and they may persist for centuries. Major decisions in education cast long shadows down the decades and the centuries, and they set a course for generations.

With such significance hanging upon them, there needs to be a means for giving issues a thorough airing and a profound assessment. The Schools Council did so in a very modest way for school education, but just how modest can be seen from a comparison of various budgets in the mid-1970s.

Schools Council	£2.5m
Science Research Council	£125m
Social Science Research Council	£12m

One would have thought that, since school education is more significant in terms of national well-being than science or social science, the consideration of its form and content merited more expenditure on it than a fifth of what was spent on social science research; or a fiftieth of what was spent on science research.

These figures have far-reaching implications. During the period of my chairmanship, one very important initiative that we launched was the Industry Project. Thinking on this project had been started by my predecessor in office, Sir Lincoln Ralphs, and we succeeded in drawing the CBI and the TUC into co-operation on a project aimed at exploring how to introduce teaching about industry into the schools.

Industry is of fundamental importance in our national well-being. In my view, it ought to rank with literature, science, history, etc., as a major subject in education for its success is a necessary condition for the continuance of our form of civilization. So the Industry Project initiative was a highly significant development.

Within the Schools Council, we pulled together as much as we could from the uncommitted part of our budget and launched the Industry Project with a budget of about £70,000 per year.

This was at a time when there was much general concern about the rather poor relationship between education and industry. A report entitled 'Industry, Education and Management' was produced with support from the Secretaries of State for Industry and for Education and Science. Its foreword reads:

> The success of manufacturing industry is vital to the country's future. The government through its industrial strategy, is committed to giving it priority over other objectives.

and it was signed by Eric Varley as Secretary of State for Industry and by Shirley Williams as Secretary of State for Education and Science.

I believe the first statement — that 'the success of manufacturing industry is vital to the country's future' — totally. The success of manufacturing industry is, in my judgment, a necessary condition for the continuance of our form of civilization.

I saw no evidence to justify the second statement that the government, and in particular the Department of Education and Science, was committed to giving it priority over other objectives. For example, compare the above-mentioned expenditure on the Industry Project of £70,000 per year with some other expenditures at the time:—

Schools Council Industry Project	£70,000 per annum
Nuclear Physics, through the Science Research Council (SRC)	£40m per annum
Astronomy and Space Research through the SRC	£26m per annum
Social Science Research through the SSRC	£12m per annum

I can recall a conversation with the Chairman of the Science Research Council at the time, Sir Sam Edwards, in which he told me — and how right he was — that our proposed expenditure on the Industry Project was an order of magnitude, even two orders of magnitude too small. So great was the need that we ought to be spending millions on tackling it.

I fully agreed. Yet all of the figures in the above table were figures broadly under the control of the Department of Education and Science. Notwithstanding their assertion that it was committed to giving industry priority over other objectives, the Industry Project, which was the most fundamental attempt then to introduce the teaching about industry into the schools, was getting only one six-hundredth part of what was being spent on nuclear physics, or one four-hundredth part of what was being spent on astronomy and space research, or one two-hundredth part of what was being spent on social science research. The figures did not convey much in the way of commitment on the part of the DES to support industry.

Visiting Schools

As Chairman of the Schools Council I had the good fortune to visit quite a number of schools. I made it a practice to visit one of the Schools Council's Field Officers once a month, and to go on a tour of schools in his area, as arranged by him. It was an illuminating and fascinating experience, coming as it did at a time when there was a growing tide of criticism of school education.

My statistical sample is of course very small, for no one individual can hope to visit more than a small fraction of our schools, but I visited nursery schools, primary schools, middle schools, secondary schools and sixth-form colleges in many parts of the country, and there are impressions that remain. One impression is what I would describe as the undistractability of the pupils. They got on with their work; they did not seem to me to be short of motivation, or of commitment, or of performance, or of enjoyment. They had a sense of application to their work, a willingness to work and a self-discipline in getting on with it which ought to put many an adult worker to shame.

I remember at the time a Member of Parliament saying that he did not believe that MPs had been serving the best interests of the country when they had been behaving like illiterate and ill-mannered school-children. I met many school children who could very justifiably have resented a comparison of their literacy and their manners with those of Members of Parliament.

It may all have been misleading. It may be that, human nature being what it is, I was shown only the best, the unrepresentative, but the adminstrators of education assured me that I was being shown fairly typical circumstances. So why was there the great tide of criticism about our schools and about the standards of education? Was it, one wondered, being orchestrated in some way, to divert attention from shortcomings in some of our other social systems? I formed the impression that schools were being unfairly criticized because of widespread disillusionment with circumstances in the wider reaches of life in our community.

There was at the time, to his great credit, a spirited defence of the schools by William Van Straubenzee, MP, who had good reason to be aware of standards in schools. In a speech at the University of Bristol in February 1977, he said:

> The truth is that there is very little really hard evidence to support the theory that standards across the country are falling. Of course, there are areas of concern, and it would be foolish to deny it. In some of our inner city areas, for example, there are fearful educational difficulties, though these often reflect urban problems that are far wider than just the school. The evidence elsewhere, and particularly in country areas, is that generally speaking standards have been rising.

It isn't the schools that create the difficult and inadequate housing conditions; it isn't the schools that generate the violence that occurs in our cities; it isn't the schools that generate indiscipline, discourtesy, and lack of respect for law and order; it isn't the schools that generate the tidal wave of low standards that are blatantly disfiguring the centre of London and most cities; it isn't the schools that generate the garish display of magazine covers that form now the everyday presentation of the wares of any book-stall, it isn't the schools that generate the lack of integrity in tax evasion or in the disgrace of a security man being moved, at trade union insistence, because he detected too many thefts; it isn't the schools that generate the callousness in many aspects of our contemporary life; it isn't the schools that preach about brotherhood and kindness but practise selfishness and indifference; it isn't the schools that create the feeling that cheating is a national disease; it isn't the schools that cause the low ebb of respect for Parliament, for money management, for industry and commerce, for justice and fairness.

One can go on, the point being that, as children grow up, they acquire the awareness of such attitudes in life outside school, from their friends a few years older, from their families, their clubs, their magazines, their television sets, their video films, and they bring such attitudes to school. Schools provide only a part of education; most education is provided by the community at large.

It is very difficult to have high standard schools in a not-very-high-standards society. The impression that I gained was of many teachers, committed to the concept of creating a civilized society through the agency of education, swimming against a tide of deteriorating standards in the rest of our social structure, against the debasement of the child by the commercial pressures in our society, and sticking to their ideals in spite of it. It seemed to me to be quite wrong to transfer to the schools a vague sense of guilt for what is happening in the rest of our social structure, and to blame the schools for it.

One would not wish to sound complacent. Of course all schools are not good, and the William Tyndales turn up from time to time to remind us of the weaknesses in the system. However, I would make a broad sweeping generalized assertion, on the basis of all the visiting that I did, that our schools are performing by and large as well as our industries and our commercial concerns. I think that they perform better than Parliament, or central government, or local government, and I am quite sure that the performance of the schools in doing their job is much better than the performance of the Department of Education and Science in doing theirs. I reckon that the rest of our social structure does not have a very strong base from which to be directing criticism towards the schools.

The Review of the Constitution

The major issue during the final months of my chairmanship of the Council was the review of the constitution, which had been pressed upon the Council by the Secretary of State for Education and Science.

The terms of reference for the review were to consider:

(i)   how the representation of lay groups, such as parents, employers, and other bodies having a legitimate interest in the curriculum, might be increased on the Schools Council;

(ii)   whether the principle that the majority of the members of Governing Council and the main Council committees (other than the Finance and Staff Committee) shall be teachers should continue to be a constitutional requirement;

(iii)   how best the effective functioning of the Schools Council might be secured both as to the operation of its committees, and as to the work and structure of its staff.

Much of the criticism of the Council centred upon the second of these. There was a widespread dislike of the majority of teachers. I must confess that the criticism puzzled me. There was no comparable criticism of the University Grants Committee on the grounds that it was dominated by a majority of dons. I found it hard to imagine an Industries Council which didn't have a majority of industrialists on it, or a Churches Council which didn't have a majority of churchmen, or a Medical Council which didn't have a majority of doctors, and so on.

The criticism was really of the teacher membership of the Schools Council being determined entirely through teachers' unions. Personally I would have preferred to have a teacher membership which was organized through their professional affiliations rather than through their unions, but the union-organized membership was a long-established system.

By and large it worked. Occasionally union attitudes and inter-union rivalries showed, but I must say that teacher members from the unions did their homework thoroughly. They made excellent contributions to debates and I sat, as Chairman, through a number of discussions in which the quality of contribution was very high indeed. It was a privilege just to be there, let alone to be Chairman.

The review was very difficult because of conflicting pressures — pressure to reduce the size of the Council, pressure to widen its spectrum of interests, and pressure to increase lay membership. Notwithstanding the volume of criticism of the Council, it seemed to me that every organization that felt it had a view to express on the school curriculum wanted membership of the Council, and we met many delegations wanting to convince us of the strength of their claims to membership.

My foreword to the Review Body's report to Governing Council read as follows:

It is the custom in our country to develop our institutions by a process of adaptation. Men alter and improve them to suit the changing circumstances of the times in which they function.

The years 1976 and 1977 have seen a great upsurge of public interest in education, a growth of interest indicating a renewed conviction that education is profoundly important. It is an indication, too, of a widely held view that education is of such fundamental significance that it must be good — a view that is unhesitatingly shared by many teachers. It is an expression of a need for a sense of assurance about our schools, and for confidence in the system whereby gradings and assessments are determined. It is an expression of a wish to see the education of our children protected against the uncertainties of pedagogical fancy and experiment, and against the instabilities of political shifts.

There is a yearning for leadership. The circumstances, national and international, through which our nation has to conduct its way of life grow steadily more complex, and call for understanding, far-sightedness, knowledge and courage. The young are going to need these qualities in greater measure than we their elders have yet demonstrated. The educational responsibility is therefore very great. The effort to enhance the development of young people is one of the most challenging of the works of men. It is difficult to accomplish it well, and it is not to be tampered with lightly. Its development calls for the highest quality of informed consideration.

The schooling of our children is one of the most significant and influential of human institutions. The quality of thought that is given to the concept of education, to its content and conduct, will affect the character and quality of our civilization for generations. The growth of public interest in education is a very welcome trend, and the review of the Schools Council, set in that context, is very timely.

We developed the idea of a Schools Council in which there was a dual structure. On the one hand there was to be a kind of Parliament of Education, which we called Convocation and on which there would be a majority of members from outside the schools, and on the other hand there was to be a Professional Group consisting mainly of representatives of the teachers who have to implement educational schemes in our schools.

My successor as Chairman of the Schools Council, Mr John Tomlinson, has often told me what an admirable structure it is, and is seen to be by those who make the effort to comprehend it and by visitors from abroad. My view was that it would need some years to get it to work properly, but it was never given the chance.

I had seen Convocation as a particularly important body provided the outside interests really made the effort to make it so. To give an example of how I envisaged it working, let me put forward a proposition about which I feel quite strongly, namely that 'Industry ought to be a Subject in Education'. Whether others agree with the proposition or not is not very relevant here. What is very relevant is that Convocation was the ideal body into which to inject such a proposition for consideration. Without a body such as Convocation there is no focal point for such general discussions of fundamental principles. Now it no longer exists.

A Summing Up

I count it a privilege to have been Chairman of the Schools Council for a brief period. For all the criticism of the Council, it was an excellent concept, and in practice it had done and achieved a great deal of very good work, and the range and quality of its publications are very praiseworthy.

The villain of the piece in my judgment was the Department of Education and Science, who emerge from it all with little credit. I would have wished that, had such been their intention, they had simply told me that they wished to see the Council wound up. I could have respected such a statement, but as it was I could have no respect for the methods which they did employ — to knock, to write a Yellow Paper, to make adverse comments, draft bitingly hostile letters, to give no support when support was needed, to undermine. I am not aware of any public assertions made by them to express support or to give defence against the flow of criticism.

It is my hope that, before the end of the decade or perhaps the end of this century, a more enlightened Department of Education and Science will re-invent the concept of the Schools Council. For all the shortcomings and inadequacies of the practical expression of the concept which existed, it is too good a concept to be forever suppressed by mediocrity of thought and lack of imagination in the Department of Education and Science.

From Projects to Programmes: The View from the Top

John Tomlinson

The destruction of the Schools Council was the saddest and most symbolic episode to occur on the education front during the Great War between central and local government (1976–?). The Council had been created in 1964 by the combined power of LEAs and teachers confronting central government. It was ended 1982–84 by an act of central government which starkly revealed the new impotency of teachers and LEAs. The weakness of the LEAs was mainly attributable to the effects of corporatism in local government, which had destroyed any effective unified national voice for education. Indeed, the contrast between the origin of two significant episodes illustrates how far the education system had been allowed to become the vassal of the DES.

In 1976 the local authority associations decided to eliminate the Association of Education Committees (AEC). They did so to remove the *imperium in imperio* of the education committee within the local authority. It also removed the single national voice for education. Whatever the merits of the decision, it was taken by local politicians and taken in the belief that local government as a whole would benefit. In 1982 the Schools Council was closed by fiat of the Secretary of State. The decision, after a little initial hesitation, was accepted by local authority politicians and all but one of the teachers associations. Yet it was these very local authorities (through the agency of their single national voice) who, shoulder to shoulder with the teachers associations, had in 1963 insisted on the creation of the Schools Council in preference to a curriculum study group set up and staffed by the Secretary of State. And it was the local authority associations, acting together after the demise of the Association of Education Committees, who in 1977 helped reform the Schools Council's constitution so that they and the DES — the joint paymasters — controlled policy. And in this they received the support of the teachers associations who, like the

John Tomlinson

LEAs, realized that times had changed and that a sharper focus was needed. And yet, only four years after this new model Council had begun operation and with the first of its widely-welcomed programme material rolling out, the local authorities accepted that removal of the government's 50 per cent of the funds was tantamount to the closure of the Council and, even more inexplicably, accepted in its stead two councils each nominated by the Secretary of State. As though this were not enough to swallow, the new Examinations Council was to be entirely funded by the DES (paymasters call the tune) and the Curriculum Committee, though jointly funded, would only be able to work on those residual pieces of the curriculum not designated by the DES as their own prerogative. As the Secretary of State put it to the Chairman of the Curriculum Committee in a letter of instruction (30 January 1984) immediately before the first meeting, 'the formulation of curriculum policy lies outside the Committee's remit.'

In stating the case thus, I suggest that the Council was destroyed mainly because it had become an obsolete expression of the distribution of power in the education system. The obsolesence had set in with great rapidity. Even in 1984, the rhetoric of central government still spoke of partnership. Sir Keith Joseph's letter to Professor Blin-Stoyle of 30 January goes on: 'I am sure that in discharging its responsibilities for curriculum development, the Committee will wish to take fully into account the curriculum policies now being developed by the Government in consultation with its education partners.' But the next sentence gives the game away: 'The most recent statement of these policies is in the speech which I made at the North of England Conference on 6 January.' Two days after that speech, in a programme for Radio 4, I congratulated Sir Keith on picking up so many of the useful ideas current in the education world. Speaking in the same programme he expressed disbelief that his proposals were not novel.

If this analysis is broadly true, it makes the final phase of the council, while I was its Chairman, of peculiar interest. The life of institutions in a period of fin du siècle is of special interest to the historian. The sense of change in political environment and of stress among former allies were indeed apparent. Yet overriding all this, most of which is visible with hindsight, was a marvellous sense, in 1978, of making a new beginning and throughout those four full years, a spirit of energy and enterprise pervaded our work. It is that which I want to try to capture, for it was the true essence of the last phase of the Schools Council.

My earliest memory of the council is the party given at Great Portland Street to say farewell to Sir Alex Smith and welcome me The

Secretary of State, Shirley Williams, was chief guest and spoke of the importance of the new-style Council. There is a photograph of four chairmen of the Council. The impression my wife and I received most strongly was of the liveliness of the staff, their cohesion, and the welcome, even affection, offered chairmen.

Once in post I came to realize how much it had cost to carry through the review and reconstruction. One Joint Secretary had left, two others left soon. Curriculum Officers, Field Officers and those in research and examinations all wanted to know how they could contribute to new policies — indeed how new policies foreshadowed in the reorganization would be made reality. The new Secretary was in post by September 1978 and his deputy by April 1979. The new committees were appointed by their various constituencies and plans laid for first meetings. Position papers were discussed and written. Meanwhile, 100 existing projects and all the examinations work were serviced by the staff.

The most novel part of the new constitution was Convocation, intended not as a governing council, but as a two-way broadcasting system for the public and the profession. We approached its first meeting with a slight sense of awe. Papers were prepared — by the members as well as the secretariat — which still reward re-reading. The room at the Wembley Conference Centre was set out for a seminar rather than a confrontation, members sat where they chose rather than en bloc, and Chairman and Secretary were at floor level not platformed. The press were near at hand, not corralled. The sense of a new beginning at a point of national opportunity was strong. John Hudson, Deputy Secretary at the DES, told us that the government was very concerned there should be no slackening of speed on 16+ examination reform now that the White Paper had been published; and that 1980 could be a turning point as the HMI secondary survey and the curriculum survey were published, and the first steps taken towards Warnock. Sheila Browne (Senior Chief Inspector) urged the Council to think about the use of teachers' time in schools, to think about the whole curriculum in schools and not to lose sight of 'simple, central educational issues.' Style would be at least as important as content, for the Council. For the first time, the voice of parents was heard (Mrs Buckley the PTAs' representative said she had never heard of the Schools Council before) and that of the CBI and TUC.

The weekly press remarked on the sweetness and light and thought it might be partly because I had made the members work hard at writing papers. The Jimmy Young programme (always a good friend to education) interviewed me that day. The daily press and radio and TV news, though notifying interest beforehand, were stampeded on the day by a row between government and TUC over pay policy.

The process towards policies for 1980–83 was now in top gear and headed in the direction of a residential meeting of the Finance and Priorities Committee in May 1979. This was the Committee given control of finance and policy with the DES and the LEAs (joint paymasters) in the driving seat.

By the time we came to the Bramley Grange residential weekend, 18–19 May 1979, the Committee had met often enough to have grown a sense of identity and I knew the members well enough to assist the dynamic. Convocation and the Professional Committee had deliberated and given strong leads. The meeting proved a great tribute to the members' spirit and stamina. They arrived on Friday evening or Saturday morning from the hectic activities of the week and all parts of the country and got down to intensive work. We took stock of how the Council's money was being spent and future commitments. Room for manoeuvre would only arise by stages as current projects finished. The priorities pressed upon us were, teacher effectiveness, individualization of learning, curriculum balance and context. We had also to consider how to organize any work put in hand and how to handle our public relations, which had often been thought too narrowly directed at only the profession.

My notes for my summing up show how well a synthesis of purpose and method was impelled by that intensive twenty-four hours. We decided to organize our work into five programme areas: the organization and effectiveness of schools as a whole; the effectiveness of teachers and methods of learning; the content and balance of the curriculum; the pupils themselves, including those with special needs; and how the whole process could be assessed, including the formal examination system. This approach would allow us to judge the balance of our work, through time, as between these five, all-embracing, aspects of the education system in a way which the individual project approach could not. It would encourage work through other means besides projects so that practising teachers and whole schools would become involved with the Council. It was predicated on the idea of a network of effort between Council, schools, researchers and the consumers of education so as to further the development of a curriculum community. And as a last flourish in that final session, such was the sense of cohesion and purpose abroad, we decided that the time had come for the Council to make its own statement about curriculum.

These 'principles and programmes' were subsequently published as a small pamphlet, partly because the importance of keeping in touch with our public had been so often pressed upon us. It led to one of those flurries of misunderstanding with the DES which were no one person's fault but which did nothing to endear the Council to the Secretary of State and Permanent Secretary and gave me the task of rebuilding bridges I had thought already well-founded. In the middle of August 1979 I was urgently called to meet senior officials. Ministers and the Permanent Secretary had received copies of the Principles and Programmes and were upset. It had taken time to convince Ministers that up to eight senior members of the DES and HMI had been involved at every stage over the past year. It was symptomatic of the jumpiness of a newly-arrived government about established processes. But it was enhanced because the government at that time did not have a clear view of what it intended. Ministers had made statements about a framework for the curriculum (for example at the SEO Summer Conference), but by that time no action had been put in hand with officials at the DES.

The decision at Bramley Grange to produce a Schools Council Statement on the Curriculum was also to prove fateful for our relationships with the DES. A curriculum study group was appointed and set about its task with great determination. Usually it met from 6.00–9.30pm after members had already done a day's work. Though deliberately kept small, it contained both DES officials and HMI. By the Spring of 1981 it was completing its work and final drafts were being circulated. I then became aware of anxiety in the DES. At first it appeared as excessive criticism of the drafting which, when probed, resolved into matters easily accommodated: only to be followed by a repeat performance. Then I was asked directly to delay the publication of the Council's document until the government had been able to publish theirs. I knew that if this got into the committee process at the Council it would cause dismay. So I took the responsibility upon myself to accept what was being asked of us. It seemed, and still seems, entirely reasonable that a major government statement should not appear to be pre-empted, even by a statement to which it is a party. We had always assumed that the Council's *The Practical Curriculum* would appear some time after the government's *The School Curriculum* which had originally been scheduled for publication at the end of 1980. Only its delay until March 1981 caused the clash. It remains of interest, in view of the criticism sometimes made of the Council, that it could not move fast enough, that *The Practical Curriculum* (which required the line-by-line agreement of half-a-dozen different interests from teachers to CBI) could be completed more quickly than a statement by government (which has only itself to please). I regretted the incident. The encomiums given *The Practical Curriculum* at Convocation on 9 April 1981 and subsequently had, for my inner ear, the ring of a tocsin.

Almost exactly a month earlier, on 5 March, Sir Keith Joseph had told the House of Commons that he had appointed Mrs Nancy Trenaman, Principal of St Anne's College, Oxford, to review the functions, constitution and methods of work of the Schools Council. The review had been planned for some time beforehand and I had agreed to stay on beyond my three year term, to allow its completion and decisions thereafter. The time allowed the Council from the approval of the new principles and programmes (June 1979) to the decision to review (December 1980) was therefore only brief. Only this period free of anxiety was vouchsafed staff and members to get on with a job which, in approaching me in March 1978, the then Secretary of State had described as of 'exceptional significance and potential.' The marvel is that so much got done in so small a compass of time. To look at the Council's bulletins as the project and programme material was published and at the programmes for conferences and training days is to see the whole range of the essential concerns of the contemporary educational scene. They are utterly relevant and were created in the crucible of practice.

Moreover, the forward thrust, once generated would have driven still further. One of my last recollections is of the two-day meeting of Convocation at Scarborough in September 1981, called to begin the process of deciding the Council's work and priorities for 1982–85. I re-learned how difficult it is for 'outsiders' to come into the context of a profession and a public service (I had first learned by serving on the Child Health Services Committee). Several — from the parents, medicine, and the media for example, — said to me 'Now I know what Convocation is for and what I can do in it, and I am invigorated'. The result of this kind of thinking and the professional and political experience of members and staff over three years produced a powerful forward plan. It not only embraced developments from earlier concerns (under-fives, the primary curriculum, the under-motivated and alienated, teacher training) but had begun to find a mode which integrated pedagogy with the society and culture in which it was embedded. As a counterpoint to the threnody of gloom about British society, we wanted the raising of the young to emphasize and draw upon the rich social and cultural capital of this society. We wanted to help create schools that were strong and stable democratic institutions, exploring how both the individual and the common life can be pursued in a spirit of freedom and toleration. For this teachers needed a new conviction in themselves founded in collegiate as well as individual professionalism and greater contact with the economic and cultural life of society.

All this was possible of utterance by a group who had met only ten times and contained the most diverse of elements. And it could have been successfully pursued through the vigour of the widespread working contacts which had been developed with the schools and LEAs on one hand and with many departments of government, and the industrial and commercial world on the other. The education service had come of age. Its practitioners not only knew they should cooperate with and sometimes share their tasks with the laity; they also knew, increasingly, *how* to do it, and were enjoying the experience.

As I conducted that last session at Scarborough I still had hopes that I would be able to hand over the chairmanship in the following December to someone who would inherit all that energy and sense of purpose and also a Council improved in its constitution by the Trenaman reforms, or something very like them. That I could not, and had to hand over to an Acting Chairman, who in his turn had to accept the decision of the government to close the Council, was the result of two forces. It seemed that the government did not want to operate within the traditional partnership. And some among the new generation of civil servants had seen the opportunity to avoid the longeurs of consultation. Parallel with the constructive work of that autumn of 1981, was the growing realization of how damaging had been the private evidence given by senior DES officials to the Trenaman enquiry — and how angry they were that it had been set aside in the Report. It looked increasingly as though their view would now be further pressed on ministers.

Matters came to a head publicly when an article in *The Times* of 3 December 1981 gave the substance of the DES evidence to Trenaman. It was 'particularly scathing about the Council's staff and Secretary. The Council required a competent, loyal and submissive staff ... but now there seemed to be serious danger of disorder through lack of control'. The contradiction between being loyal (to the Council's decisions) and submissive (to the DES), and what the 'danger of disorder' really was have never had to be explained or justified. At the special meeting of the Finance and Priorities Committee on 3 December I had to use my skills and the corporate identity of the Committee not to educational ends but to deciding how to deal with this attack on the Council. All interests represented were concerned and outraged. HMI (who had contributed so much to the work of the Council) could only sit silent and DES officials tactfully stayed away.

At my meeting with the Secretary of State on 10 December I expressed the grave concern of the Finance and Priorities Committee at the 'evidence' given to Trenaman. My notes of that meeting will serve as my epitaph for the Council. The Council's underlying concern was that the Secretary of State should appreciate that curriculum development was not like most other academic or industrial research. It needed not only ideas, but action. It needed the wholehearted support of the LEAs and teachers for its success. They must therefore be committed to its purposes and methods and that would only be achieved by involving them in its creation. A nominated body, as proposed by the DES, would face unnecessary difficulties in achieving this kind of motivation. The Council had also asked me to put their views on four other particular points. They had the utmost confidence in the management and organization of the Council. The teacher associations on the Council did not act there as trades unions, but as professional associations. The DES and LEAs had a majority in the Finance and Priorities Committee. The new objects and methods of the Council were still developing. From my viewpoint as Chairman I added that I thought the educational system as a whole was the better for having a place where its elements met to do something constructive, rather than only confront one another over salaries, conditions of service, rate support grants, and the like. I also urged that the full potential of the changes wrought in 1977/78, with improvements possible following Trenaman, had still to be realized. Finally, I emphasized how strongly I thought that the elements for a new style curriculum-cum-assessment-cum-teacher training system were to hand.

I started this account by identifying the underlying historical forces which were inimical to the Council. It was killed off by a change in the environment rather than through inherent weakness. But such generalized movements cannot solely of themselves determine events, particularly events such as which quango should survive (the FEU, the HEC) and which be cut down (the Schools Council, the Family Committee, ACACE). The detail is determined by the personalities and interests of the individuals concerned who — depending on your theory of history — either become the instruments of the zeitgeist or seize their opportunity to further virtue as they see it.

During the four years, I was conscious of two categories of critic: those who disliked the Council and took every opportunity to do it harm; and those who wanted it to succeed and regretted both its own foibles and the increasingly hostile attitude of government.

The political dimension at the DES and the way in which it changed over the four years is easily discernible and I doubt if an insider's view adds much. At the beginning, Shirley Williams had every intention of making the DES role in curriculum and examinations more forcible, but was also keen to use the new form of traditional instrument placed in her hands by the 1977 review of the Schools Council. When I discussed with her the aftermath contemplated for Circular 14/77 (the DES's first catechization of LEAs about their responsibilities for curriculum) and warned her that I would want the Schools Council to be given a big (not exclusive) part in remedying identified deficiencies, she replied 'Don't worry. We haven't put you there to do nothing.' The General Election of 1979 brought Mark Carlisle to the Secretary of State's chair. He inherited and developed the drafts of government curriculum statements. He was also the first Secretary of State to have the courage to take decisions about a common 16+ examination and broadening of 'A' levels. He had to accept an external review of the Council because of the Pliatsky report on quangos in general and because a review (though not external) was proposed by the Council itself in the 1977 shake-up. Had he remained in power, it seems possible that Trenaman's recommendations would have been accepted. That he was removed is indicative of the wider determination to change things. Sir Keith Joseph was eventually persuaded that advice on examinations should be directly under his own wing and to emasculate national advice and activity for a co-operative kind of curriculum.

The post-1977 Schools Council constitution contained a fatal flaw. The DES were represented by officials. All other members were virtually plenipotentiary. Local authority members and officers, teachers, parents and church and industry representatives could all join in debate and contribute to the development of ideas and decide on the spot whether or not to support the outcome. Civil servants by contrast came with a pre-agreed line based on the papers for the meeting. Faced with the burgeoning of ideas and proposals during a meeting they became isolated and felt at a disadvantage. In the former Council they could blame the hegemony of the teachers associations for decisions reached. In the new Finance and Priorities Committee they had chosen to share responsibility with the LEAs, and the senior civil servants who were party to that change had fully intended to play their part. But as the attitude of their political masters changed they could participate less and less.

What should have been proposed, and may still have to happen in the late eighties, is a Council in which ministers join on equal terms with LEA and teacher leaders to get certain kinds of debate and agreement. Beyond that, each constituency must have its prerogatives. The mark I Council recognized no-one's prerogative and skewed power de facto.

The present situation invites continual war between the king and his barons. Eventually, if we wish to avoid despotism, we must come to the king in Parliament for education as we did for other purposes some time ago. The Mark II Schools Council remains the best model so far devised.

From Projects to Programmes: The View from the Inside

Don Cooper

"If it were done when 't is done, then 't were well
It were done quickly:......"

Macbeth

And so the change from Projects to Programmes was done quickly. In such a way would the problems besetting the Schools Council be resolved. A change of constitution followed by a change in emphasis in ways of working was going to be the panacea — or so it was hoped.

In July 1979, following a residential conference of the new Finance and Priorities Committee, the document, 'Principles and Programmes' was published. In it were the outlines of the five proposed programmes of work. By September of that year planning groups were in being, by the end of the year fully costed proposals had been prepared. Early in 1980 the new Council committees considered them, and in April 1980, the programmes were launched. Designed to cover the Council's work for the following three years, except of course for existing work on projects previously funded, the programmes began a new era for the Council.

For many of the staff, preparing and implementing the programmes was a time not only of excitement and challenge, but also of extreme pressure — writing papers, preparing for meetings, writing numerous proposals, organising conferences, arranging for consultants to be available, and above all meeting deadlines. A new-found confidence and optimism began to fill the corridors and committee rooms of Great Portland Street. Doubts about the wisdom of preparing programmes in such a hurry were put on one side. After all, new opportunities were emerging not only in the way in which curriculum development activities were to be mounted, but also for the Schools Council itself. Successful programmes emphasizing partnership, particularly with LEAs, could give the Council a new and prolonged life.

From its foundation in 1964 the Schools Council had been a responsive agency in the way it had allocated funds to curriculum projects. Requests for the funding of curriculum work were received by the Council, considered by its committees and, if approved, became the Council's projects. Usually the applications, often prepared meticulously, came from experienced educational research workers who were adept at writing proposals, and often understood extremely well how to adapt their proposals to suit prevailing requirements. Usually too these curriculum developers were based in universities or colleges and planned their projects on the assumption that the problems they were addressing were the ones facing teachers in classrooms or the ones that teachers ought to be facing in classrooms. Very often they used teachers to try out and help develop the materials that were produced, sometimes with outstanding success, but once produced, the materials usually became the new expertise, and were fed to teachers through commercial publishers on a take it or leave it basis. Where projects did produce materials that teachers found relevant to their own problems and needs, they took them, often adapting them to meet their own special requirements. On too many occasions, though, the teachers left them, and as a result the word *dissemination* became very important.

So important did dissemination become that many projects, originally funded without any strategies for dissemination, returned for further funding. Unfortunately, this further funding did not seem to solve the problem of poor take-up, and soon there was sufficient concern for the Council's committees to commission a major project to examine in detail the impact and take-up of past and current projects. Not content with that the Council, to its great credit, decided to take a lead in self-evaluation, and set up a review body to examine its own constitution and ways of working. As a result the constitution was revised, the committees reorganized, and with the coming of programmes, methods of working were altered. For the first time in any major way the Council initiated work without waiting for outside agents to submit proposals. No longer did the teachers' professional associations have a majority on all the committees; the existing three Joint Secretaries were replaced by a single executive; liaison groups were set up to accommodate the interests of parents, higher and further education, and the world of work; and Council staff began to play a far greater part in planning and developing curriculum work, thus contributing their professional expertise much more fully than had been possible in the past. After fourteen years the winds of change were blowing very strongly — they had to if the Council were to survive its growing number of critics.

Perhaps the most significant change came when the 'new' Council decided to establish its priorities, and then to use most of its available funds to initiate work on those priorities. As a result the programmes were born, each having a thematic title and a more specific remit.

The details were:

Programme One

Title: Purpose and Planning in Schools

Remit: To concern itself with how schools decide their curriculum aims; plan their curriculum; relate to the world of parents, governors, the local community and to employment; organize links with other schools and institutions; prepare for change; organize themselves; and acquire the requisite managerial and interpersonal skills.

Programme Two

Title: Helping Individual Teachers to Become More Effective

Remit: To be concerned with patterns of learning and child development; learning styles and skills; teaching styles and techniques; teacher-pupil interaction; diagnostic assessment; the assessment of children's learning and progress; and self-assessment by the teacher.

Programme Three

Title: Developing the Curriculum for a Changing World: Developing Basic Skills and Preparing for Life after School

Remit: To be concerned with improving children's grasp of certain basic skills: verbal communication, numerical, graphic, logical, scientific, study, and social and personal. The programme was also to be concerned with

helping pupils prepare for life after school, promoting
education for political and economic understanding,
education for life in a multicultural society, vocational
choice, technological awareness, environmental issues,
and outdoor pursuits.

Programme Four

Title: Individual Pupils: Identifying Talents and Needs, Responding to Problems and Dealing with Difficulties
Remit: To identify talents and respond to the needs of children
with special education requirements; those who opt
out, including disruptive and truanting children; those
from ethnic minorities; and gifted children.

Programme Five

Title: Improving the Examination System
Remit: To develop fairness, accuracy, and uniformity of standards across the examination system; and to develop
better school leaving report systems for all pupils.

In other words the programmes were intended to cover almost all
the current educational problems. However, what was extremely interesting was the language used to introduce these programmes:

The curriculum is shaped by the influence of teachers, local
authority advisers and officers, HM Inspectors, initial and
in-service trainers, examining boards, and many others.

The Council believes the base for development will be streng-
thened and much more achieved if it works in partnership with
other central and local, public and private agencies.

In particular the Council is committed to supporting local
curriculum developments.....

Principles and Programmes

What was being proposed was indeed a radical way of working for
the Council. What had happened to the curriculum developers of
former projects? Had they been relegated to the 'many others' in the
first quotation? And yet the words seemed to echo those of the late

Derek Morrell, one of the Council's first joint secretaries in whose name the Morrell Fund had been established. This fund was set up to help teachers with small local curriculum development work on problems they had identified. Administered by the Council's Field Officers, the Morrell Fund had been retained under the revised constitution, and indeed the principles underlying it were used as a basis for Programme Two's network activities. Derek Morrell had spoken in the 1960s of engaging the active participation of large numbers of teachers as well as the participation of other agencies. In the Joseph Payne Memorial Lecture in 1966 he described the Schools Council as being the central organ of the professional democracy which he felt was needed, and went on to suggest that this democracy should be locally organized bringing together teachers, dons, administrators and others for the study of common problems, some local and others national. Describing this approach as expedient, he continued:

> This wide involvement of teachers and others in the work of curriculum development . . . has however, a deeper significance than mere expediency. Certainly it is expedient: no other procedure would be likely to promise a shorter time lag between the phases of development and of general application. But it is equally necessary if the work is to offer support to the teachers in the anxious business of responding to change, to respect the quality of their present efforts, and to help them decide for themselves — from personal conviction — what changes are needed. . . .

If only these words had been heeded earlier. But some thirteen years later the Council was being urged to work in a similar way for a second time. How did it respond?

In the autumn of 1979, programme planning groups came into being. They consisted of committee members and senior Council staff. Each contained DES, HMI, and LEA representatives together with members of professional associations and Council staff. Their task was to produce carefully-costed programmes of work covering as far as possible the remit given in Principles and Programmes. Here at last was a chance for real partnership in action. There were no caucus meetings before or during planning sessions by groups with vested interests, no 'assessors' or 'observers' from HMI or DES representatives, at least not overtly, and no differentiation between committee members and staff. Instead, in the two planning groups attended by the writer, individuals worked side by side sharing their knowledge and their expertise freely with others in a spirit of genuine partnership; and when the groups needed expert help, they were able to co-opt experts to their ranks or use them on a consultancy basis. Each curriculum planning group held a three-day conference when the bulk of the detailed work was undertaken, and these were so successful that by the middle of December 1979 it became obvious that each planning group would produce its programme on time.

Even so, many people involved had reservations. The fact that costed proposals giving details of process and products were required placed a severe constraint on at least one planning group which wished to concentrate on the processes of grass-roots curriculum development where although the theme might be suggested by the programme, the actual problems to be addressed were to be those encountered by practising teachers. How could products and process be described before the problems had been identified? In such a situation the whole idea of a fully-costed proposal in the generally accepted sense is almost impossible to deal with. Eventually, that planning group compromised by preparing costed proposals, but referred to them at all times as 'models' and not actual proposals. Thus in practice, the models could be amended, altered, or even ignored when the real problems became apparent. But even these models were not achieved without difficulty. To prepare them the group split into two. One half prepared its proposals, the other did not. Deadlines were near and the only solution was for the staff of the planning group to meet and prepare the missing proposals. This they did on a wet Friday afternoon with the help of one of the group's co-opted members who arrived thinking erroneously that a full planning group meeting was taking place on that day. Fortunately, he was very experienced in writing proposals, and did in fact prepare three that were later accepted by the planning group as having a high priority. Even so, writing proposals in such a way did not seem to be the ideal way of preparing for the future.

Another limiting feature, which only became really significant at a later stage, developed as a result of the way in which the programmes had been organized. There were no cross programme links at committee level or indeed in any significant way at staff level although programme directors, once appointed, did meet regularly to discuss matters of common concern. These meetings usually dealt with administrative matters and rarely with the content of the programmes. As a result, programme chauvinism developed affecting some committee members and staff alike. The consequence was that opportunities for co-operative effort were missed.

A further constraint was the shortage of resources, financial and human. Approximately £50,000 was allowed to each programme in the first year, with about £150,000 in each of the two subsequent years. This would have been just about enough to fund three major projects for each programme under the old style of working — the remit of each programme had to cover far more than could be covered by such projects. But the shortage of human resources seemed to some to be an even bigger constraint. Each programme was staffed by a Programme Director who was, and indeed remained, notionally, a half-time appointment, a full-time Executive Officer to deal with administration, a half-time secretary, and some occasional clerical assistance. As the programmes developed, two of them appointed full-time Assistant Directors to help cope with the increasing work-load, but even those appointments were barely sufficient to cover all their needs. After programmes had begun, support groups were set up to help Programme Directors and to facilitate the flow of information which the programmes were generating. These groups consisted of staff from the various sections of the Council. But these members also had their own jobs to do with the result that support group meetings were usually held monthly when Field Officers visited London. Even so, the help of the support staff was invaluable.

Despite all the limitations the programmes started work in April 1980, Programme Directors having been appointed from full-time Council staff some three or four months earlier. What was achieved?

The programmes developed idiosyncratically from the start. Each adopted a different strategy for coping with its remit. What follows is an account of one programme's work and its attempts to carry out the tasks it had been set. Concentrating on one programme's activities does not imply that it was more successful than the others. Indeed, all programmes had their successes and failures, but the experiences of the writer as a Programme Director contribute to the following account.

Programme Two, 'Helping Individual Teachers to Become More Effective', was designed by the Planning Group to focus on the professional development of teachers. Having struggled with the concept of effectiveness, the Group decided to concentrate on certain key principles which were articles of faith about how teachers do become more effective. These principles were to underpin all the activities of the programme and came to be known as the programme's philosophy. The principles were that:

- activities should focus on the individual teacher's classroom work;
- teachers work best on problems they have helped to identify;
- teachers become more effective when encouraged to appraise their own practice and then to consider different methods of working;

- working in partnership with other teachers, with LEAs and with other agencies helps teachers with their professional development;
- research undertaken by teachers into their own teaching is an effective way of promoting curriculum development;
- teachers' professional development is an integral part of curriculum development.

Given this philosophy, the programme adopted two main methods of working: it was responsive, making small awards, usually of up to £500, to networks of teachers and others who sought help with problems they had identified; and it commissioned work on themes within its remit. In all, there were 109 activities: ninety-seven small-scale, often the result of local initiatives, and twelve commissioned by the programme. These activities were based in colleges of further and higher education [28], LEAs [25], universities [19], schools [15], teachers' centres [11], and subject groups [8]. There were also three evaluation studies based at Schools Council. All these activities were on themes developed by the programme, and details of these are given below together with the number of activities which identified themselves with each theme:

Patterns of learning and child development	24
Learning styles and skills	55
Diagnostic assessment	17
Assessment of children's learning and progress	49
Profile reporting	11
Teacher-pupil interaction	41
Teaching styles and techniques	59
Teacher self-evaluation	57
In-service education	66
Dissemination	40

The appeal of this method of working for small-scale activities was evident not only from the numerous enquiries received, but also from the very favourable comments made to the programme's independent evaluator who surveyed the teachers' opinions. The cost effectiveness of this method of working was also reported by the evaluator commissioned to report on all the programmes of work. One activity, which received an award of £500, was costed in real terms, and the value was put at almost £15,000. The other advantages of giving small-scale grants were that:

— work was generated by the programme on its specified themes;

— teachers and advisers were supported throughout the country, not just in selected areas. In all there were groups working in seventy-seven LEAs;

— the image of the programme was enhanced because local groups recognised that the programme was concerned with their problems and also valued their work;

— potentially valuable ideas were supported at an early stage and thus encouraged to develop.

Much of the programme's commissioned work also emphasized the role of the teacher as a major partner. Sefton LEA and the City of Liverpool College worked closely with teachers to develop diagnostic teaching techniques and activities. In Bath, teachers evaluated curriculum materials; in Norwich they investigated children's thinking; in Manchester the emphasis was on studies of assessment procedures; and in Nottingham and Cambridge teachers worked on problems associated with project and topic work; in Wales the problems were those concerned with profile reporting; in Lancaster on teaching methods suitable for vertical grouping; and at the Open University on in-service materials for the teaching of reading. In East Anglia there were several groups of teachers working on the problems which arise in teaching for examination success, particularly when those teachers are concerned about teaching for understanding.

Although the production of materials and reports was not considered as important as engaging teachers in the processes of curriculum development, nevertheless the programme's activities did produce numerous products. Some, usually involving in-service materials, are being published commercially, and several reports have been published in the Longman series of programme pamphlets. Other activities have decided to produce their own reports and materials making them available either nationally or in their own areas. Even these products reflect in the main the philosophy of the programme — they are not designed to become a new expertise. Instead many are intended to stimulate further action on the part of teachers to encourage them to examine their own practice in collaboration with their peers. This is seen as full teacher participation in the processes of curriculum development, school-centred, active, and person-oriented.

So what has changed or been changed? Comments reaching the programme's staff indicated that change had been perceived in various ways. One comment from an observer who had had contact with the Council over a number of years dealt with the change of language he had noticed. In the days of projects the key words were: target-populations; teacher-proof packages; impact; RD&D; centre-periphery models; and analogies with cafeteria systems. With the advent of programmes the key words became: negotiation; consultation; networks; social interaction; teacher autonomy; action research; participation; and partnership. It is interesting to note that the second group of words mirrors a different strategy for curriculum development which requires a change of attitudes, relationships, values and skills. Implicit in that strategy is the belief that teachers can be active agents in their own learning and development. It was with this approach that major parts of the programmes were concerned.

Another change was noted by a professor of education who was being urged to adopt the principles of one of the programmes. He remarked after a while that 'working for projects was never like this in the old days'. He went on to say that for projects one received a grant, and then one could get on with the job more or less unhindered. Having to adopt principles of working was a totally different proposition.

But perhaps the greatest contribution that programmes made was to show how important small-scale activities could be. Originally, there had been suggestions that giving small awards was like throwing pound notes to the wind. Once the full potential of such awards had been realised that criticism disappeared. Indeed, had the programmes been able to continue their work, these local groups would have provided sufficient knowledge about the problems they were addressing to generate future work for scores of teacher groups.

It is probably unfair to pass judgment on the overall success or failure of the programmes, particularly as they had to work under the threat of the Council's closure, but they certainly represented a different style of working. The available evidence suggests that some of the greatest strengths of the programmes were that they addressed practice, that they supported grass-roots development, that they actively encouraged partnership, particularly with LEAs, that they indicated future development work, and that for many of the staff involved with them, they were personally and professionally rewarding. Unfortunately, with the closure of the Council they were cut off just as they were in a position to make an even greater impact.

And so the panacea failed to materialize for the Schools Council, as it had failed to materialize for Macbeth.

From Projects to Programmes — The View from the Sharp End

Jean Rudduck

My own professional biography, from 1965 to 1983, has been signi-
ficantly shaped by the changing structures, aspirations and fortunes of
the Schools Council. During the early years I was a member of its first
in house research team; then, during the golden period of the curriculum development movement I joined one of its high-cost, high-risk
projects; and during the last years I directed several of its small-scale
projects — the last of the summer wine. Although I have a long view of
the Council, it is not an overview. At each point in my series of
engagements with its work, my own focus was narrow: I was concerned
with interpreting and pursuing the task in hand. I cannot paint an
official portrait: all I have is a collection of snapshots, personal and
partial.

It all started, I think, with an HMI inspection of the school where I
was teaching. The then Staff Inspector for English seemed to enjoy what
was happening in the classrooms he came into — although I can only
remember one swirling, frenetically participatory exploration of the
Pied Piper of Hamelin — and shortly after (the two events may not, of
course have been related) I received an invitation to an international
conference for young teachers. There, as often happens at conferences, I
lost my professional innocence: there were worlds outside the classroom that I had not dreamed of where fundamental educational ideas
were examined and disputed, and where experiences were shared and
criticized in a spirit of intellectual excitement and commitment that was
new to me. After the conference I was as bewildered as Bottom the
weaver: 'The eye of man hath not heard, the ear of man hath not seen,
man's hand is not able to taste, his tongue to conceive nor his heart to
report what my dream was'. I applied for a job at the newly-established

Schools Council for Curriculum and Examinations — and was offered it. In such ways are promising teachers lured from the small, secure island of their school and — also like Bottom the Weaver — translated. (The curriculum development movement was of course to be another translator of classroom teachers — a sort of Trojan Horse in reverse). I didn't go back to the classroom.

I had been a lively teacher with good classroom control and a delight in and respect for my subject, and would have succeeded for a few years on the energy and optimism of youth, but I had no real foundation of professional understanding that could have carried me dynamically and effectively into mid-career. That's not such an uncommon situation, and what teachers like me look to then is the support of the staged novelties of PSRs (posts of special responsibility) which can, sadly, prevent the deepening of pedagogic insight by offering incentives to move up the managerial ladder. My PGCE course had provided me with the basics but basics are never enough: the training failed to equip me with ways of looking at and thinking about the events and interactions of the classroom as a basis for the improvement of my art as a teacher. Having sloughed off the thin skin of theory that I prudently acquired as protection against the summer examinations I had no impulse to continue with the formal study of education, and I had no framework which could lead me to question my own implicit assumptions or that explained the workings of my small world. And then, one day, I met the Schools Council! Even then it wasn't exactly an overnight conversion.

The Council had advertised for young teachers to form a research team under the leadership of Philip Taylor (who all too soon deserted us for the Chair in education at Birmingham). It took a long time for the Council to work out — having decided that it was proper, or prudent, to have a research team — what to do with it. There were three of us on the top floor (no lifts) of 38 Belgrave Square: David Shoesmith, Roland Harris (a not-so-young teacher) and myself. We had no real research experience and were given no research training but we knew that policies were evolving, and a certain sense of privilege at being part of something new enabled us to cope with our role uncertainties. Our main responsibility was to attend subject committee meetings (I of course, was allocated to the Home Economics Committee) where we kept our heads down until we realized that no one else knew what to expect from the research team either!

We were also linked to a number of enterprises that were relevant to the Council's developing understanding of its own identity and ambitions. For instance, I visited the North West Regional Development Group where, under Alan Rudd's careful and encouraging leadership, teachers in different subject areas, across schools, met regularly to work out their own courses of study using the then novel framework of Bloom's Taxonomy of Educational Objectives (later I became a renegade and handed out car stickers that said 'Help Stamp Out Behavioural Objectives'). I was impressed by the support for collaborative planning that the objectives model offered and recognized the power and fruitfulness of working through teacher groups. I was also attached to a group of Sheffield teachers who were writing up their experiences of school-based CSE assessment.

There was an air of speculative adventure and the climate was receptive to individuals with vision. Charity James, from Goldsmiths College, for instance, came knocking on the Council's ears: she was energetic, enveloping, confusing, but she had something that made teachers excited and that seemed to be what mattered. We also had our own internal charismatic figures. One afternoon, on the second anniversary of the Council's birthday, Derek Morrell, one of the Joint Secretaries, called all the staff together in a large bay-windowed room overlooking the Square and addressed us. Our research team secretary commented: 'He makes you believe in it even if you don't understand what it's all about'. That was true. We entrusted the future to the Joint Secretaries — Morrell, then Caston and Owen, and these were people whom you respected and whose visions you waited, patiently, to share.

I can't point to anything that I contributed of any particular significance during my time at the Council, but the work that I valued most was with the government social survey and led to the publication of *Enquiry 1: Young School Leavers*. I took part in pilot interviews, in the structuring of interview schedules, and was present at some of the briefings of the cohorts of (mainly housewife) interviewers. The work was confidently and meticulously managed by Roma Morton-Williams and it was a good introduction to survey research. My involvement in *Enquiry 1* was also important because it focused my serious attention on the problems of preparing for the raising of the school-leaving age — the arena for my next period of employment with the Council.

The contracts of the research team were short-term. After two years I took up a post as Senior Lecturer at Brighton College of Education. I remember dropping my letter of application into the pillar box in Belgrave Square and then trying awkwardly to retrieve it. The post was in English, not in education, and in many ways it was a wrong move. I continued to tie up work I'd been doing for the Council while I was there and after about seven months, as I sat in my rather bleak black and white linoleum-tiled study, one of the Joint Secretaries rang me and asked whether I would consider applying for the post of schools liaison officer on the Humanities Curriculum Project — a project which was to be funded as part of the Council's programme in preparation for the raising of the school-leaving age. The feasibility study was carried out while I was at the Council and its approach hadn't attracted me. 'No', I said. 'Why not go up for an interview?' he said. 'Well, it's a free trip to London', I thought, so I went — and in a sense I never came back. Lawrence Stenhouse, the Project's Director, collected me in an old green Jaguar from Victoria station. Geoffrey Caston moved courteously to the back seat. No small talk: they continued their discussion, ignoring me, until Geoffrey was dropped at an underground station. My resistance was intensifying! Lawrence interviewed me — in a coffee bar in Park Lane — and all doubts evaporated! This was another man of vision: articulate, inspiring and confident. Again, I didn't understand or grasp the significance of what he was about — but I responded to his values and to his commitment. I joined the Humanities Curriculum Project Team in April 1968. My responsibility was to act as link between the team, LEAs, and schools, and to organize project conferences. This was when I learned most about education. I was now part of a team which had a task, which had money to meet the needs of the task, and which had time to think about the task.

Concern about the raising of the school leaving age was building up and LEAs and schools were receptive — indeed they were impatient to get at what we had to offer. Each week the HCP team took a whole day for a full staff meeting. This seemed at first an unpardonable extravagance given the demands that were being made of us, but it was the time spent in discussion that united us, that gave us, over time, a shared understanding, and that provided a supportive forum for the intellectual and practical uncertainties and difficulties that we were facing. We learned to trust each other and that proved important given the battering that we were to face, individually and as a group, as a result of the Project's challenge to the established order of things.

Our autonomy as a project team was considerable. We kept in touch with our sponsors through working party meetings (where we largely determined the agenda) and through the close intellectual companionship of our Project Officers (John Banks, then Paul Fordham, and later Ian Parry) who took time to involve themselves in our problems and learn alongside us. We were able — and had sufficient resources — to gather together, for additional consultation, a group that came to be known as our Critical Friends (members of our sponsoring institutions, the Schools Council and the Nuffield Foundation, were part of this group); we also had a number of whole day or half day meetings with philosophers and experts in group discussion and classroom observation to help us reflect on the epistemological and pedagogical underpinnings of our work. The big projects were after all advancing along relatively untravelled paths: in addition to developing a coherent experimental pedagogy we were discovering, documenting and analyzing problems in the relationship between central team and trial schools; problems of curriculum implementation; problems of materials production and censorship; problems of evaluation in a non-pre-specified objectives model of curriculum development; and problems of designing and managing training workshops for teachers that were process-oriented and not materials dominated. The Council's policy was wise: they gave us our head and they gave us support. This was the best way to proceed, for in those pioneering days the Council could only learn about curriculum development by observing and reflecting on what its project teams did.

In 1969 HCP was at the peak of its activity: it was a time of subtle shifts of direction and responsibility as the demands of dissemination intruded on the continuing demands of development and support for trial school teachers: we were throwing a new set of balls into the air while trying to make sure that we didn't falter in the existing routine. We had gained additional funding for a time extension of the project by establishing that dissemination and evaluation were integral parts of project design, and we were working out ways of managing the tasks of dissemination and evaluation that reflected the complexity of the project and the resources and receptivity of its potential users (a 'training the trainers' strategy in dissemination and a 'briefing decision-makers' strategy in evaluation). Council staff continued to be closely interested; they were still in a 'big is beautiful' frame of mind and there was concern to ensure that the experience and insight of project team members was not lost to the system when the project ended. Institutionalization was the answer — in what was called 'Centres of Excellence'. (Opponents of the institutionalization principle argued, with some justification, that people with such experience and insight should get back into the system as soon as possible and try to lift it from the roots.) The Council's Joint Secretaries started negotiations to place the HCP team in a university setting and in 1970 we moved to establish a new Centre at East Anglia. Tenured posts were offered to a core of people whose presence on the project was required right up to its end in 1972 and who wished to stay on: Lawrence Stenhouse, Barry MacDonald, John Elliott and myself. The four of us, although tenured, accepted the fact that we were expected to find our own salaries out of research and development grants. We expected the Council to commission us, since they had sought to establish us, but at this crucial moment they turned their back on us.

It didn't of course happen quite as suddenly and starkly as that. Over time personnel changed: Morrell died in 1969, Caston left in 1970 and Owen in 1968. The period of expansion and bold curriculum speculation was over, and the values that one regime was committed to, the next was not obliged to endorse. The balance of power shifted from inspirational leaders to committees and it's not easy for a committee to develop a corporate charisma. The Council was now in its first review and consolidation phase.[1] It seemed to be more wary, more cautious — and more suspicious. At least, it was highly suspicious of the Humanities Project. HCP was conceived at a time when the Council was committed to a policy of extending the range of choice open to teachers and it tried to do just this: not only did it offer a rigorously thought-through alternative course of study in the humanities, but it also offered alternative conceptualizations of the process of curriculum development. 'No curriculum development without teacher development' was our slogan and we saw the teacher's engagement with the project, even at the point of dissemination, as 'participation in an experiment'. People who did not grasp the logic of this position, nor appreciate the strength of its underlying commitment to the professionalism of teachers, saw it as arch, precious, paradoxical and irritating. Moreover, HCP was undoubtedly disturbing many teachers and the press didn't miss a trick in reporting the views of its castigators. Where, earlier, controversiality might have been perceived as a mark of a project's effectiveness in generating and sustaining worthwhile debate about fundamental issues, now it was treated as something of an embarrassment and nuisance. Caston offers an explanation of this shift. HCP was by no means the only project to question 'the effectiveness of the traditional didactic authority role of the teacher', and he comments: 'All this was not particularly palatable to the teacher union establishment which was increasingly exercising the control over the Council's decision-making which the constitution gave it. Professional associations and unions are rarely in the vanguard when roles are being redefined!'[2]

The most bitter confrontation, for us, came when one of the Council's committees vetoed the publication of the project's materials on race relations, negligently disregarding, so it seemed to us, the research evidence of our own pilot study, and of other studies, which suggested that an approach through open discussion might be an effective means of deepening understanding of multi-cultural issues and thereby of increasing tolerance. (We later learned that the committee members were to some extent victims of an adverse publicity campaign deliberately mounted in the popular press to ensure that the project lost public sympathy.[3]) Relations between the project team and the Council were strained, to say the least, and from then on we received only minimal support from our sponsors. In our view the Council was becoming over-managerial, less concerned with the quality of ideas than with the smooth and successful passage of its projects through the system.[4] 'Take-up' was the newspeak; our fundamental concern with making an appeal to the professional judgment of teachers seemed, in comparison, a sentiment from a more leisured era. During the lean years of our relative neglect by the Council we struggled in small ways to keep the ideas of HCP alive and to ensure that the pedagogy that was their vehicle remained accessible. It wasn't easy. I submitted a proposal for additional support for dissemination. It was summarily turned down. Later I submitted another, for interest among schools was still strong, and I knew that less controversial projects were being generously supported in their 'after care' activities. This time I was invited to attend the meeting of the committee whose task it was to consider the proposal and make a recommendation to a higher, decision-making authority. The proposal was turned down on grounds that revealed more prejudice than understanding and, incensed, I made a direct appeal to the new Chairman, John Tomlinson, in terms of the Council's stated policy of ensuring that alternatives were available in the system. My appeal resulted in an over-riding of the recommendation not to support the proposal. That was a turning point in our relationship with the Council.

My colleagues at the Centre for Applied Research in Education (CARE) now grew more confident about climbing out of the trenches and approaching the Schools Council to reestablish a working relationship. I was the one nominated to carry the white flag. We sensed that Lawrence Stenhouse was still seen as too maverick to be trusted - one of the 'gifted but sometimes wayward people'[5] who were appointed directors of the early projects. I submitted a proposal in the area of in-service which grew out of our work on the dissemination of HCP. Out of respect for the 'value-for-money' line of defence that the Council was then having to take in the face of mounting criticism, the project was called: 'Making the Most of the Short-Inservice Course'.[6]

The Council's structure for control over this project was quite different from what I had known in the days of HCP. My in-service project didn't fit into any of the existing topic or subject-bounded committee structures. I was given (or given to!) a small, stable Monitoring Group which was purpose-built for the project, which met regularly and was prepared to immerse itself in the data. In the days of HCP, trust in the Project Director was the basis of the funding and the foundation of the Director's subsequent autonomy; now, trust was something that had to be built up, collaboratively, over time. I found both approaches comprehensible and acceptable. The members of the Monitoring Group — Michael Henley (CEO) Chair, Jack Chambers (teacher and NUT), Arthur Clegg (HMI) and Don Cooper and Freddie Sparrow (Council staff) — enjoyed (literally) a high level of debate; meetings were always stimulating and I think we all looked forward to them. By the end of the project, members of the Monitoring Group understood it sufficiently well to take an active role in presenting it at dissemination conferences. The interests and expertise matched the needs of the project remarkably well and their contribution was considerable — but this degree of support and understanding was bought at the cost of the time and attentiveness of several busy and senior people. The one project/one Monitoring Group formula was effective — but probably not efficient except as a one-off strategy.

In the Council's next phase — the Phase of the Five Programmes — the structure for support and control was different again and, in my view, much less effective. I was funded by Programme 2 to coordinate research by teachers into children's thinking. One Committee was responsible for all the projects and activities that were given grants from the Programme 2 budget. Although a 'major' project in terms of our budget (approximately £18,000) we met the Programme Committee only once during the Project's lifetime (and once to discuss the report) and then only as one item on a crowded agenda. Now Programme 2 had at its core a set of complex and radical principles relating to the idea of teacher-as-researcher and to the idea of teacher groups linked into a network and representing a significant force for change within the profession. Don Cooper, the Programme Director, knew the implications of the Programme that he had conceived, but I doubted whether the Committee members ever arrived at a shared understanding of the principles that lay at the heart of Programme 2 and that should have given it a powerful coherence and identity. The Programme spawned a profusion of projects and the Committee seemed, understandably, concerned to get everything into print as a testament to its vigour and to its generosity to teachers. The Programme's field officers, whose task it was to maintain links between the Programme Committee and the projects, had heavy loads, and intimate involvement was prohibited; moreover, the values of Programme 2 virtually obliged the field officers, on their official visits, to sit in on, and therefore validate, regular meetings of the Project's teacher groups rather than debate with project coordinators the important issues that Programme 2's work was exposing. In such circumstances I doubt whether either field officers or committee members could ever grasp what individual projects were about if they aspired to any subtle or sophisticated exploration of the process of teacher research. We had interpreted our task as helping the Programme to explore, in practice, the implications of its rhetoric. We committed ourselves to examining (a) the process of teacher research and relationship between teachers and a university-based support team; and (b) whether new and worthwhile ways of looking at teaching and learning would emerge if teachers, rather than academics, were given (i) the task of defining the precise focus of enquiry; (ii) the role of researcher; and (iii) the responsibility to theorize about their data and present their insights to other practitioners. The first draft of our Report, which gave equal weight to the content and to the process of teacher research, was met with a fair degree of impatient scepticism. In the second draft, with a severe word limit, the discussion of process had to be compressed into a single, final chapter. The Report was accepted for publication but in the second division pamphlet series: we failed to make the glossy paperback series that projects with our level of funding aspired to. But that perhaps is all that we deserved.

My feeling at the end of the Project on Children's Thinking (which coincided with the end of Programme 2 and the end of the Council itself) is that the potential of Programme 2 to make a unique and significant contribution to our understanding of the principles and practice of teacher research had not been — indeed, could not be — fully achieved. In trying to explain to myself why this is so I find myself looking back to our experiences at the end of HCP, and there are some similarities in the two situations. *First*, in both situations power was invested in committees and the vision of the individuals who had conceived the goals that guided the Committee's work was not something that committee members could grasp without patient periods of collaborative intellectual enquiry. Committees cannot deal in dreams; they have to deal in practical action and their procedures have been evolved in support of this responsibility: for example, they work to an agenda of disparate items that require quick shifts of focus; then there is their size, the infrequency of their meetings, and their limited meeting time. If committee members are not appointed on the basis of their known understanding of and support for a particular set of principles then it is hard, if they are to complete their business, to build common ground. Look behind the rhetoric that appears to bind a committee to its task and you often find an alarming degree of intellectual disarray.

Second, in both situations, the Council was concerned to prove itself in the face of criticism. In the first phase, security was sought through consolidation, and in its last phase (I speak only of the Programme with which I was associated) security was sought in the trophies of productivity — long lists of teacher groups that had received support and long lists of publications; these celebrated the ranging energy of the Programme but did not contribute to its intellectual coherence. (The task of making sense of it all now lies with the person appointed to evaluate Programme 2, Gordon Bell, but his Report, when it emerges, may well be a case of unlocking the stable door after the horse has lost all desire to bolt.)

In a sense the Council has continually faced the problem of trying to make creative the tensions that have existed between its different and sometimes contradictory impulses and commitments: for example, the tension between autocracy of vision and the democracy of committees, which I have alluded to above. But there is another tension, equally significant, between grand central initiatives and, modest support for local activities.

The early period of the Council's life witnessed a change of scene: the curriculum development dinosaurs (as they have been disparagingly called) lumbered off the stage and a troupe of school-based in-service and curriculum initiatives came scampering on. The departure of the big projects was, in my view, a real intellectual loss. Their central teams had the time and money — and freedom — to tackle fundamental pedagogic issues in ways that were beyond the scope of school-based teacher teams whose members have a full teaching load. The price of local relevance is often lack of pedagogic coherence and rigour. I sometimes see the 'school-based' curriculum movement as an artful device for preventing radical curriculum reform from sweeping across our schools with the force of a real bid for change. Of course, radical thinking will be self-generating in some schools but by no means in all — and it is unlikely to spread effectively on a wide scale.

The pendulum of Council policy has never swung right away from the big 'central team' initiatives of course (they survive in areas of greatest concern such as schools and industry and secondary science, in itself an interesting comment). But what characterizes the work of the Council's final phase is probably what Programme 2 represents: the apotheosis of the ideal of 'benign support for local initiatives.' Groups pick up and receive nourishment from the small but numerous amounts of money that have been scattered broadcast up and down the country. And animation is important, for with teacher mobility at a low ebb a stimulus was sorely needed that would direct teachers' attention back to the classroom and to pedagogy. Professional staleness can set in early during a period of retrenchment — as teachers in Programme 2 activities made clear:

> I'd got to the stage where I wanted to think a bit more about what was going on in the classroom. I have been teaching now for three years and I sort of felt I needed something to interest myself in.[7]

For such teachers, the opportunities provided by Programme 2 were a professional pick-me-up, offering the incentive of a small grant; a task; an opportunity for focused professional dialogue; the promise of publication; and a sense of being in touch with the wider educational community. What we cannot tell easily is the impact of this involvement on the quality of their professional thinking and on the coherence of what Bruner has called the 'deep structures' of their curriculum planning.

There is, I think, a way of reconciling the seemingly contradictory impulses of centralized and localized curriculum development. The key is research. Teachers are probably better at classroom research than they are at school-based curriculum development, and what research competence offers teachers is a means of enabling them to get a critical grip on ideas and materials offered by central development projects. As Lawrence Stenhouse said of the curriculum projects he directed and that he saw as offering teachers 'evidence' to help them construct their own responses: 'Using research means doing research' — in other words, a proper response to externally designed curricula is research-based implementation. (See a parallel argument used by Illich[8] in relation to 'science for people' and 'science by people' and the mediating power of a 'critical technology' that helps teachers to make intelligent use of what so-called 'experts' offer who are distant from the realities of everyday living).

My experiences in Projects and then in Programmes leads me to question whether the Council did enough in its early days, in relation to its Projects, to ensure that the consumers were developing a sufficiently critical response technology. Halpin (1966) said that the 'real dissemination task is to increase the "literacy" of the consumer'.[9] I suggest that the Council (given its vulnerability to public opinion) has sometimes preferred to dilute the challenge of its thinking in order to meet the expectations of its consumers rather than to raise their expectations. It failed, perhaps, to see the significance of the tensions that its changing policies exposed between individual vision and democratic control and also between central team curriculum design and local group curriculum activities.

Acknowledgement

I am grateful to Gordon Bell for letting me see copies of his interim and draft final reports on Programme 2.

References

1 NISBET, J. (1971) 'The Schools Council, United Kingdom' in (1973) *Case Studies of Educational Innovation I at the Central Level*, CERI, OECD.
2 CASTON, G. (1975) 'Epilogue' in BELL, R. and PRESCOTT, W. (Eds) *The Schools Council: A Second Look*, London, Ward Lock Educational, pp. 162–66.
3 WINTER, G. (1981) *Inside BOSS: South Africa's Secret Police*, Penguin.
4 RUDDUCK, J. (1980) 'Curriculum dissemination as planned cultural diffusion' a paper given at the AERA conference, Boston.
5 CASTON, G. (1975) *op. cit.*
6 RUDDUCK, J. (1981) *Making the Most of the Short In-Service Course*, Schools Council Working Paper 51, London, Methuen Educational.
7 HULL, C., RUDDUCK, J. and SIGSWORTH, A. (1984) *A Room Full of Children Thinking*, Longmans for the Schools Council.
8 ILLICH, I. (1981) *Shadow Work*, Marion Boyars.
9 HALPIN, A.W. (1966) *Theory and Research in Administration.*

A Schoolteacher's View of Schools Council

Margaret Raff

I was one of the lucky few who could, and frequently did, by catching trains and 'cutting it fine', arrive at meetings of the Schools Council, literally, straight from the classroom. I was even luckier to be able to test out, in practice, the curriculum ideas we had developed in Committee meetings and working parties; and prove or disprove their validity. That's what I'm going to miss most of all with the death of Schools Council. I think, too, that what the government will also miss (though whether or not they'll be upset about this is open to question, of course) will be the almost total lack of input from the grassroots, from those people who are not afraid to venture opinions. There's nothing more half-baked than people theorizing about what can and ought to be done with youngsters in the classrooms, whether it comes from the DES, LEAs and their Advisers, college and university lecturers, retired headteachers — and all that rich panoply of people who believe they know about education. They may or may not have fine ideas — but the real problem nowadays is translating new ideas into the practical processes of getting young people to learn in an ambience which includes: teacher colleagues who are dispirited, suspicious, resentful and angry; fearful of their jobs from falling rolls and with no prospects of improvement to their status or real income; who are hostile to the increasingly centralist authoritarian stances of the DES and LEAs (the 'Teaching Quality' White Paper *must* have been written by someone who is abysmally ignorant of these moods, for it is so openly contemptuous of teachers and the efforts they are having to make in doing their job). A pupil population in many cases, comes to school from home backgrounds which no longer value or believe in education as a passport to an improved way of living, let alone as something for its own sake and, in its adolescent years, is either vociferously condemnatory of what's on offer — or merely passively indifferent which is, in its way, even worse. Mind you in these respects they could be right, for the examination system which dominates our lives in school is so constraining, unimaginative, dull, obsolete and incredibly irrelevant to the real world of mass youth unemployment. I feel sorry for our youngsters who have to rotate the examinations treadmill. I feel even sorrier for myself, though, at the prospect of not being able to bring about changes, especially when I listen to some of the examinations enthusiasts now occupying privileged and separatist positions in the Secondary Examinations Council. At least in the Schools Council, because there were tenuous links, we were able to expand their narrowness and rigidities and oblige them to look at the real world of curricular and vocational pathways and whether or not what they were proposing was useful evaluation and had pedagogic validity. Now there is no democracy, no accountability, no testing, no validation — NOTHING — that is in the least responsive to anything that I and hundreds of thousands of teachers like me do or say.

Despite the best — and more probably, the worst — intentions there can be no substitute for the continuous hands-on experience of, and daily interaction with, classes of youngsters to pose and answer the question 'Can it/does it work for me?'. With all due deference to my Headteacher colleagues, advisers, HMI — even full-time teacher union and TUC spokespersons — even if you once taught youngsters you can soon forget what it feels like to cope with the job of teaching dissatisfied or disgruntled school leavers. You cannot retain, even recall, the sense of weariness you carry out of school at the end of the day at your inability to motivate those young people with the present examinations diet — and for me it was my participation in the work of Schools Council that gave me hope and optimism for change — that there were prospects of 'light at the end of the tunnel'. Why?

Because there I met leading and influential people, key decision-makers from the educational world, who not only were demonstrating sympathy and sharing appreciation of the problems I was identifying and the practical strategies being advanced for change, but were in a position to engage in dialogue, mutual listening and learning. That was so important! They had the ears of people who mattered and could and did take decisions and spend money. But what do we have now? Look at TVEI! We have delivery systems that deliver money and criteria. We have LEAs encouraging competing bids between departments in schools; between schools and schools within limited areas of LEAs and between area consortia of schools within LEAs. Inside the schools we have some youngsters who are school haves and the rest who are the have-nots. This model, which delights the DES and the Manpower Services Commission (MSC), has dangers for us all — not least the educational process — the teachers' raison d'etre — for what is emerging is what we had learned to spot and play down at the Schools Council, and that is the 'bolt-on' approach as a substitute for curricular change. Where's the evidence of massive cross-curricular consultation, exchange and rationalization? Precious little if any. Yet we were insistent upon the importance of organic change from and by the institution itself, as a fundamental pre-requisite. We talked about inter-curricular development within the schools. Perhaps we *were* too laissez-faire in the ways we operated, but, at least, given the skinflint levels of budgeting and the microscopic amounts available to each school and its teachers, plus Schools Council's total inability to assert, direct and control, we achieved far more *real curriculum development* in terms of the *teachers* we influenced (who are after all, the only real delivery system for any curriculum change). Certainly the bolt-on approaches that can now be seen have all the potentialities for compounding the resentments referred to earlier — for positive attitudinal changes don't respond well either to bullying or bribery.

In the light of that, and upon reflection, it might not seem so extraordinary after all, that just as so many excellent and effective links were being made with further education, the MSC, with representatives from both 'sides' in industry, let alone the good working relationships developed, as I thought, between representatives of the teachers, the LEAs, HMI and the DES — down came the hob-nailed boot (wrapped in sacking to deaden the sound) which scrunched to lifelessness all those splendid initiatives.

There was such a great deal of intellect, commitment and practicality brought to bear, for instance, in the two main committees on which I served — Professional and Secondary Curriculum — for they were always lively, entertaining and very task focused. I'm sure they made most people feel good about education in England and Wales. Certainly to judge by the incredible responses and take-up of our ideas, and their practical implementation at local authority — even school-levels, we were talking the kind of language that teachers in the schools understood and were ready to introduce, despite their shoe-string budgets.

There were some hard debates too, about curricular directions — especially over the notion of the introduction of skills and competencies into the practical work of the schools, especially secondary schools. Our discussions sharpened the cutting edges of ideas which, otherwise, would have stayed at the lofty abstract level of so many conferences which I've had the misfortune to attend, in other spheres of activity.

The major weakness of the Schools Council, which I believe we were on our way to curing — or, at least, making a perceptive analysis over — was that it had no real delivery system. Everything depended on good faith and belief in the inherent willingness of people to do the right thing.

Schools Council participants were brilliant at setting aims, but not at defining goals, even less at prescribing curricular objectives. But small wonder for the Examinations Committee was a separate entity divorced from the curriculum work. It had a lifestyle and influence of its own and, therefore, set the agenda for the real work of the schools.

I know now that you cannot change the curriculum without, in tandem, developing evaluation strategies to be used to test whether your curriculum design, learning objectives setting and teaching methods are appropriate.

We had moved towards that position in the Secondary Curriculum Committee; we were trying to bridge that gap, but that gap was still apparent in the Professional Committee where the Examinations Committee had an elitist indifference to most of the other issues that were talked about. They had the real power.

I think it's naive of some people to talk of the new Secondary Examinations Council and the even-newer School Curriculum Committee as being 'successor bodies to the old Schools Council'. They are not, nor will they or can they be, for they have reinforced and institutionalized those same ridiculous deficiencies that marred our work in the Schools Council.

Nonetheless we were moving towards a point of gaining the trust and cooperation of teachers. Had we had more money, more staff and the ability to organize and arrange INSET and staff release (in the way that, for instance TVEI can and does) we would, I believe, have become profoundly and democratically influential in curriculum development in schools. I believe that the current Government's thinking was/is deeply antipathetic to that, certainly some of its administrators are and that's why the growth of networking that was developing had to stop — it was passing out of central control and direction and into the hands of the teachers. The entire process has now been reversed.

But teacher autonomy and its resistance to dictation and prescription appears in many guises and, as the government and its supporters in the LEAs have found, the teachers have been giving vent through the agency of the 3 per cent salary straw that broke the camel's back. There is now no way that teachers will be intimidated into accepting or operating an agreed curricular framework, validated by an external examinations system, that doesn't allow them to respond, flexibly, to the demands of their students. Whatever the current Secretary of State (or any future holder of that office, as he is prone to say) thinks about the maintenance and use of corporal punishment the 'short sharp shock treatment of offenders' offers neither remedies nor results. Neither will increased computer-time if there are no jobs available in high-tech industries in the local job market. Our school leavers, let alone their parents, are not going to be fooled. Only a socially and locally relevant educational/learning programme will be, otherwise they will carry on increasingly doing what they are already, ie. voting with their feet.

The assumption that consultation with LEAs means schools and, even more teachers is maddeningly naive. Any consultation process over the curriculum must be followed with a development and review process too. But can the present government satisfy and resolve the deep suspicions that are now manifest throughout the system. I doubt it. I think the credibility gap is now too wide. Any form of partnership that doesn't assert its priorities and its hierarchies in terms of who is doing the work? Who gets most tired at the end of the day? Who is at the delivery end? Who has most to cope with? Who has to be most flexible? Who has to introduce modifications and variables in response to human need and development? Who stands no chance of working effectively?

The prime failure of teacher training in this country is its inability to recognize, deal with and develop the importance of teaching and learning skills. It is, in fact, *shameful* (I use the word quite deliberately) that the new developments of core skills in work-based projects for Youth Training Schemes have not come as a by-product from the education system but from industrial training. Yet caring, social and life skills, communications and problem solving are all part and parcel of a teacher and her pupils' work. But university professors on ACSET still hold forth and assert their priorities and status over others for a General Teaching Council (or its substitute) for England and Wales. The government still feels it can ignore the teachers' professional organizations and consult its own hand-picked Headteachers and LEA functionaries in preference to those who are representative and accountable.

Teachers, on the whole, have friendly, albeit somewhat amused and patronizing, memories of the Schools Council. But they weren't afraid of it and they were ready to be influenced by it (if they thought its ideas would work). But what a dreary prospect faces us now in the schools. We need something to hope for that will bring relevance and change into our work. What has the government to offer in place of what we had?

Another LEA View

Joan Dean

I miss the Schools Council. I miss the programme committees and the working groups and all the various occasions when one had the chance to meet and talk with and learn from people whose experience was different from one's own. As a member I had a feeling of being part of national development, part of a network which the Schools Council brought together, a network now sadly in pieces.

Eric Briault in his paper describes the early days of the Council. By the time I joined we were into the period of falling rolls and falling expenditure, the period when education started to be under threat and criticism. My first aquaintance with the Council was in the early 1970s, when I was invited as one of the representatives of the National Association of Inspectors and Educational Advisers to a meeting of the working party concerned with dissemination.

This working party had been set up because of the concern being expressed about the lack of impact of some of the major pieces of work which had been undertaken. A number of ideas came out of this study and were recorded in the published report. One idea, which was not only taken up but is being continued with the new Curriculum Committee, was that LEAs should have a contact person for the Schools Council, so that the channel of communication was clear. Another idea was the development of exhibitions of Schools Council materials in different parts of the country. There was also a move to do more which came from actual work being undertaken by teachers, sponsoring activities which were already under way which had implications for a wider audience.

I joined the Schools Council as a member at a point of change. I joined as a move was made from the idea of three Joint Secretaries seconded from their normal work for a period, to the first and last permanent Secretary, John Mann, who came bringing a clear view of the possible path for development of the work of the Council.

It was an exciting point to become involved and we spent a great deal of time thinking out how we would work on the four programmes which had been agreed. I was initially a member of Programme Committee 4 which was concerned with individual pupils.

At the early meetings of this Committee we identified four areas of work — pupils with special needs; disruptive pupils; pupils from ethnic minorities and gifted pupils. These areas of work are very different in kind and at an early stage we broke up into groups to work out in detail the programme we wished to develop, finally producing a total programme which covered each of the areas.

When work on the programmes was started I moved to Programme 2, which was concerned with teacher development. This Committee was very competently chaired by Michael Henley and supported by Don Cooper of the Council's staff. It was a very productive Committee and I believe its demise is a considerable loss to the education service.

We set out to fund small pieces of research and development which were concerned with improving the work of teachers, rather as the Dissemination Working Party had envisaged. We saw what we were doing as complementary to local initiative and funding and none of the grants we gave was very large. We made it possible for a number of pieces of work to develop at a time when the financial constraints were beginning to bite and each meeting involved hearing about particular projects from those involved in them. It was an exciting programme and those of us who were fortunate enough to be on the receiving end, learned a great deal which was of value and were in a position to disseminate information about a wide variety of work.

At the very end of the Council's life I was part of the Committee which produced the book *Primary Practice*. This group had to work hard to complete the task in time. Although we were remarkably united in our views about what was important in primary education, we had some difficulty in getting such a large topic into a publishable form, since there was so much to be said. Fortunately John Mann decided to act as writer to this group and it was largely as a result of his work that we completed a book which has been very well received by primary practitioners everywhere.

My own involvement with the work of the Council was as a representative of my professional association. I was also unofficially a representative of the LEAs because of the post I hold. I was therefore always concerned to see our work from the viewpoint of the LEA and particularly that of the advisory services.

The LEA adviser had an important gate-keeping role at all stages. Very often it would be the adviser who brought a project to the attention of teachers, sometimes setting up work and providing some LEA funding and sometimes simply making it known. This function of the adviser was well recognized.

A less well-recognised function of the advisory service was that of providing the overview that advisers get of the schools. Teachers can speak with authority of their own school and classroom and teachers' association representatives can speak of what their fellow members tell them, but an adviser can speak from first-hand experience of what is happening in a very large number of schools and classrooms and is in a position to express the views of a large number of teachers.

LEA education officers also have an overview, but this is different from that of the adviser and is quite properly more slanted towards the elected members and heads than towards classrooms. Both views are needed. The teacher majority on the Schools Council often found this aspect of the role of the adviser difficult to accept and more use might have been made of this kind of expertise.

The role of the LEA has been important throughout the life of the Council. LEAs are in the first instance the employers of teachers and the providers of resources. As such they too had a gate-keeping role and this was bound up with the role of the adviser. The adviser might determine the value of a particular project for the LEA and advise on whether or not schools should be encouraged to take it, but the adviser needed to convince the administration and the Education Committee that funds were needed.

In the early days of the Council when large projects were the fashion, LEAs adopted projects which they felt would be useful and worked with the project teams. This often involved considerable commitment from advisers and teachers and in some cases the appointment of LEA staff and the provision of funding from the LEA as well as the Schools Council. Sometimes the project took off in the LEA and remained after the team had departed. Sometimes the project gradually died out when the team had finished their work. A good deal turned on how much the running of the project was costing and whether the LEA could continue the necessary funding and support. It also turned on how well the project staff matched the teachers with whom they were working. Unless the teachers concerned were able to work without the support of the project team and the advisory service by the time the project finished, the development was unlikely to be sustained.

Later when there were many more small projects and more coming from work actually started on the ground, the function of the central body was more that of selecting those pieces of work which had wider implications, supporting them through funding and dissemination and monitoring their progress. In this context the LEA's role, along with staff from further and higher education, was to bring to the notice of the appropriate committee work which was under way which might be of interest and to continue it.

During the life of the Schools Council many changes have come about as a result of falling rolls, financial constraints and changing public opinion. It is no longer possible to start out on a substantial project and know that LEA support can be maintained until the end of it. Some teachers have become disillusioned about curriculum development, feeling that the task of managing to keep going from day-to-day is enough in itself. Money is no longer available for additional resources, whether the resources of people or materials. Public criticism of education, often ill-informed, acts not as a spur but a cause of stress for many. The former trust between the professionals in education and the parents, elected members and the public is disappearing and this makes the work of teachers even more difficult. At the same time there are people all over the country who are managing to rise above this situation and achieve developments in spite of the lack of time and other resources. One of the sources of support for much development was the Schools Council.

Towards the end of its life the Schools Council became viewed with suspicion by some outside the schools. The views which created this suspicion are still with us. There are in fact two views held by those who are critical of our schools. There are those who think that everything was better yesterday, in spite of the fact that yesterday's schools helped to produce today's problems. They take the view that schools need to concentrate on the basics and should forget about curriculum development. There are others who feel that change is not happening fast enough. Development in the world outside is more rapid than in the schools and children are not being adequately prepared for a changing world. This view accounts for the Manpower Services Commission (MSC) developments. Sometimes these two groups seem to be saying the same thing because both are dissatisfied with schools as they are.

Why was the Schools Council closed down? No-one could say that it was a matter of saving money, since the Council's budget was always very small for the size of the education service. It at no time bore comparison with the proportion of total expenditure any large firm would expect to put into research and development.

At the time when closure was being discussed, I wrote to my MP to protest. He happened to be one of the MPs who had been involved in setting it up. In his reply he made it clear that it hadn't done what was expected of it. He also said that mine was the only letter he had received in protest from his constituency. Both of these points give food for thought.

I suspect that the politician's expectations of the Schools Council which he was expressing, would only be achieved in a country with a centralized education system, if at all. It could, nevertheless, be argued that the effect of the work of the Council in the schools has not been sufficiently widespread.

Yet it is possible to point to many developments stemming from the Schools Council which have had very considerable impact. How many first and infant schools have remained unaffected by Breakthrough to Literacy? How many junior and middle schools have not heard of Science 5–13? How many comprehensive school geography teachers have not heard of Geography for the Young School Leaver? Some projects of this kind have had a remarkable impact. It would be surprising, given our decentralized system, if the freedom our teachers have to make decisions about the curriculum did not result in some deciding they did not want to use the work which was being done, although it is more disturbing to realize that this is more likely to be a decision by default, where the teacher is unaware of the work. It will be interesting to see whether the new Committee is any more successful.

Another quite different point might be made which was probably not in the minds of those who decided to close the Schools Council. If the Council was set up to reconcile curriculum and examinations, it was not entirely successful in spite of valiant attempts. The reasons probably lie outside the Council. If a single body was unable to do this there seems even less hope that it will happen with the new organization in which there is a deliberate separation of the two.

Perhaps a much stronger reason why the Council came to an end is in the change in the climate of the times. In came into being at a time when we were expanding, saw things positively and believed in ourselves and the possible effects of education. It was closed in a time of retraction, when the more negative view of education described above prevailed, along with a much more paternalistic attitude on the part of government, who seem to be saying 'we know what's good for you'.

Another criticism which might be levelled at the Schools Council was that although 'experts' were used in the projects themselves, too little thought was often given to expertise in forming working groups and committees. I described earlier the two programme committees of which I was a member. I enjoyed both and was glad to have the chance to be involved in them, but my presence on the first was chance, due to where I and other people were sitting when the allocation of people to committees was made. My fellow LEA members were sitting together and I was on the other side of the room. They decided among themselves which committee we would each join and I fell in with their decision. There was no discussion about what each of us might have to offer to each committee and as it turned out I was the only person on the Committee with any experience of work with gifted children.

I believe this was symptomatic of some of the weaknesses of the Schools Council. We should have been more concerned to harness the expertise we had among the Council members, and perhaps less concerned with ensuring that the appropriate numbers of teachers from each association were on each committee, irrespective of the particular contribution they might each make.

The Schools Council, while unique in bringing together the various groups of people involved in the education service, had the disadvantages of democracy in that you don't necessarily get the best solutions to problems by working with large committees. Some other countries make much more use of experts than we do and they may be right to do so. This isn't to deny the importance of teacher involvement. It is the combination of the teacher's knowledge of children and how to help them to learn with expert knowledge of curriculum and subject area which we might expect to produce the results. The Schools Council tried to achieve this and partially succeeded, but I suspect that the balance of teaching experts and curriculum experts was not always right.

We might therefore have expected the move to a nominated Curriculum Committee to change this balance but this doesn't seem to be the case. The new Curriculum Committee is still representative of the various interests, even though the Secretary of State has decided on the membership rather than the constituent bodies. It is difficult to know what has been gained which could be set against what has been lost.

Perhaps another omission in the work of the Council concerns the elected members of local councils, some of whom were among those who came to view the work of the Council with suspicion. Should we have done more to carry them with us? We were, after all, often asking elected members locally to support the work of the Council. On the other hand it is only recently that the curriculum has been seen as the responsibility of local councillors. For a large part of the life of the Schools Council it would not have been seen as appropriate to do very much to inform elected members about curriculum.

The life and death of the Schools Council covers a very interesting period in educational history. It is hard to remember now that none of the early work of the Council was concerned with the curriculum as a whole. We tended not to think in these terms. The word curriculum was scarcely used in the primary sector in the 1960s, though this is hard to believe now. In secondary schools the concern was, and to some extent still is, with a collection of subjects which may or may not add up to a coherent whole. It is only since the Ruskin College speech that we have been generally concerned with the whole curriculum, although the Schools Council was working on aspects of it earlier.

There is much in the work of the Schools Council of which we can be proud. It brought together the various interests in education and enabled them to work together in fair harmony. It was highly productive in many fields, some of which will have lasting effect. I suspect it will eventually have to be re-invented.

The Politician's View

Christopher Price

This chapter does not attempt to be a definitive political judgment on the Schools Council. I am not qualified to make one; and I suspect that, in any case, that judgment must come later. Rather it is a series of retrospective snapshots by an educational journalist and politician who watched, spasmodically, the Schools Council saga from birth to death.

My connections with the Council were always peripheral, and in many ways quite coincidental. My first Headmaster, in the years of teaching before I launched into politics, was Dr John Stroud, the Head of King Edward VI School, Southampton — a somewhat high church Quaker who later did a stint as one of the joint secretaries of the Council before the Alex Smith Reformation, when it was still under tripartite administration. My second, and only other, Headmaster was Arnold Jennings, at Ecclesfield Grammar School, one of the more potent influences on the politics of the Council, who ended up as Acting Chairman and senior undertaker, presiding with dignity over the various legal and procedural obsequies of its long slow death. When the tripartite secretariat collapsed, I was happy that the Council went to my old city of Sheffield to find John Mann, its first Chief Officer. I felt the City must have prepared him well, though I never knew him when I was active there as Deputy Chairman of the Education Committee in the early 1960s. I encountered many other Council bureaucrats, but fewer teachers who were active in curriculum development — which was never a subject I mastered. So if I now comment on the Council, it is as a theatre critic who knew one or two of the actors rather than as a participant who understood the play.

Apart from knowing some of the *dramatis personae*, I was also aware of the Council in three other capacities. First during two brief periods as a quasi-minister. I spent two separate years (1966–67 and 1976–77) acting as errand-boy (Parliamentary Private Secretary) to

Secretaries of State for Education and Science. During my first stint, under Anthony Crosland, the Council was new — recently set up by the drive of Derek Morrell within the new Department, with support from the local authorities and acquiescence from the teachers, once they were assured of their built-in majority to ensure control of the curriculum. At that stage, in the DES, concern to promote the reorganization of schools predominated over a desire to influence what was taught in them. The walls of the secret garden were still intact and the curriculum was left to the teachers and others within it. I heard little of the Schools Council and certainly no questions or criticisms. Educational expenditure was rising, curriculum development was an unquestioned benefit and the Schools Council a favoured quango.

During the second period, under Fred Mulley, when the whole educational machine was coming under strain, questions were beginning to be asked about the Council's responsibility for the health of the school curriculum — which was not delivering many of the goods it had once seemed to promise. The teachers in general and the NUT in particular tended to be blamed. But the Schools Council wasn't alone; the whole educational establishment was coming under siege. Mr Callaghan was surreptitiously ordering his Ruskin speech to be prepared — outside the suspect Department of Education — because he felt the education card was rapidly slipping from Labour's hands. Scapegoats were being sought. From that point onwards, the Schools Council was bound to be an obvious candidate for scrutiny and reform.

Then there were my journalistic contacts. Though Edward Boyle had warned me off education on the grounds that it was the graveyard of politics, it was, I discovered, in the 1960s and the early 1970s, a nirvana of journalism. There was plenty to be written and lots of space in which to do so. When I was still in Parliament, I edited *New Education*. When I lost my seat in 1970, I had other journalistic opportunities, both in print and on television. To me as a *reporter* of the education scene, the Schools Council impinged in a different way. My abiding impression is of endless paper, the rationale of which, try as I might, I could never fully understand. Perhaps that was a wrong impression; or perhaps a great deal of paper was inevitable. At least it is an indication that people are writing things; and perhaps it proved the claim which the Council has always made — that more teachers were being involved in the curriculum process than ever before. At all events, it failed to make me a curriculum development addict; the impression of an undigested paper mountain persisted in many other journalistic minds; and not enough was done to rebut it.

During this period many of those who wrote material for the Council wanted greater publicity for their efforts; but there wasn't much material which deserved it. What there was tended to be written by folk who found difficulty in communicating exactly what they were trying to say. In the event, the proof of the Schools Council pudding was not, in those days, in the eating of it. It neither generated a group of writers intent on interpreting curriculum development to the wider world nor threw up the charismatic chalkface of teachers one might have expected. The shape of the school system continued to grab the headlines; what was taught within it remained largely a mystery.

I would have liked, as a journalist, to have charted the progress of a seminal educational animal — realizing how important contact with the Council was to many a teacher who wanted to make some positive input into the curriculum. Indeed from time to time I did. In specific subject areas, like classics and geography, I was happy to see the Council breathe new life into many teachers who had come to something of a standstill in their teaching and were not quite sure what to do next. The same seemed to be true of history. Where it seemed to me that the Council was markedly less successful, was in transforming the curriculum from the excessively subject-based animal they found it to a more integrated experience. They tried with science; Nuffield was already in full swing when the Council arrived on the scene, in effect, sharpening and separating the edges of the new physics, chemistry and biology. As a result, it seemed that the Council's Integrated Science Project would never make much impact on the schools generally. It was much the same with the Humanities Project — the Council's attempt to make history and geography and social studies more coherent and meaningful to what Sir Keith Joseph now chooses to call the 'bottom 40 per cent'. But it got sucked into inevitable disputes about race, which it was never possible for the crude committee structure of the Council properly to resolve. I am sure it had some impact in the schools; but reporting centred on wrangles between Lawrence Stenhouse and Max Morris about the degree of anti-racist commitment which teachers should employ in the classroom. It proved a useful catalyst for promoting discussion of an important educational issue; but I'm not sure how much it advanced curriculum development.

I am sure many important curricular stories went unreported; and that this was partly the journalists' fault. But if, during this period, the journalists were never quite able to translate the excitement of curriculum development to the educational world at large, the Council bore much responsibility too. Throughout the 1970s, it withdrew deeper and deeper into its own private language. One of the reasons why it died in

1983 was because it had neither projected itself coherently enough nor coopted sufficient allies a decade earlier.

My third contact with the Council was the most substantial. It arose through my chairing, between 1979 and 1983, the Select Committee on Education, Science and the Arts. It began disappointingly. Right at the start of our investigation into the secondary school curriculum and examinations, we paid an informal visit to the Council. It turned out an awkward and unsatisfactory occasion. The culture gap between MPs and curriculum developers was such that no real *rapport* grew up between the Committee and the Council. Perhaps that would have been asking too much; and it was better when the Council came to give evidence to us. They brought along a strong and familiar team — apart from John Tomlinson, the Chairman and John Mann the Secretary, there was Jim Deboo of Baker Perkins and the CBI, Ron Cocking from the NAS/UWT, Alistair Lawton from the County Councils, Peter Horton, my successor in Sheffield, and Arnold Jennings, my old Headmaster. In the event Arnold was the most plausible and impressive witness — putting forward as eloquent a plea for integrated science as I'd ever heard.

The session transformed the Committee's attitude from wary suspicion of a dangerously trendy quango into a sort of acceptance that there was a job to do and that some reasonably independent body was necessary to do it. So when the time came to frame the Report, the existence of the Schools Council was not at issue. We just assumed it would continue.

I suspect the Committee were influenced on two accounts. First Nancy Trenaman had just completed her review of the Council, and, to everyone's surprise, had come down broadly in favour of retaining it as it was. Since Mrs Trenaman was regarded as a personal friend of the Prime Minister — like Janet Young, in that rather special 'Oxford' female category, which she valued as an antidote to the clubby male-chauvinist society in which she found herself. Indeed the Conservatives on the Committee rather assumed that since Mrs Trenaman had blessed it the Prime Minister must also have done so and that the Council had been granted an official, good housekeeping seal of approval. So they did not hunt it down, as I had rather expected them to.

There was another incident which warmed even the most right-wing Conservatives on the Committee to the existence of the Council. The minutes of a meeting that took place between DES officials, local authority representatives and Mrs Trenaman about the future of the Council were leaked to the Select Committee. They made it clear that one of the DES officials had made some deeply damaging remarks about John Mann, the Council's Secretary, without chapter and verse to back them up and without, of course, John Mann having an opportunity to rebut them. Since the DES official who we deduced had been conducting the campaign against John Mann in private, had also made a thoroughly bad impression on the Select Committee when he appeared to give evidence before it, that also, ironically, raised the Council's status in Conservative eyes. So if there was a plot to blacken the image of the Council and to get an all-party Committee of the House of Commons to suggest its abolition (a scenario that could have been engineered) it never got off the ground.

I also misjudged the situation. I had fondly imagined that the Trenaman Report would have settled the issue; and though the government might have cut the Council, I thought it highly unlikely that its existence was in any jeopardy. I had understimated the rapacious determination of the government to obtain ministerial control over the school curriculum. Thatcherism in its most intense form had not quite materialized in 1982; the Council had not been abolished in the first attack on quangoes in 1980. In retrospect I should have realized that it was at greater risk. Though the Select Committee couldn't have saved the Council in the face of Sir Keith's determination to abolish it, we could have analyzed its position more carefully and put more positive recommendations for its future in our Report.

What precedes is an anecdotal account of the impression the Council made on me over its lifetime, especially in the realm of curriculum development. I now come to the harder and more overtly political issue of the examination system. When the work of the Council is reviewed by future historians, it will, I suspect, be the Council's failure during its period of office to alter the shape of the public examination system in England that will be accounted its greatest failure. It would be wrong to blame the Council too much for this. Whereas, until very recently, politicians have been reluctant to interfere in the curriculum — largely because they do not feel competent to do so, they have always regarded control over the examination system as one of their prerogatives; nor do the politicians have a monopoly of either interest or control in the examination system. The universities, the CBI, the civil service and a host of other local and national interests want to be consulted. The existence of a vast 'examination board' industry makes changes very difficult.

All that said, however, the Schools Council, during its lifetime spent an enormous output of money, time and energy on the examination system and its reform. Quite properly. The more intelligent of its officers always realized that the English curriculum is 'examination-led'; all the curriculum development in the world can go on, but if at the end of the day the CSE, 'O' level and 'A' level remain as they are, it is those examinations which will fix the fundamental nature of the curriculum more or less immutably from generation to generation. That is why there has been so much more curriculum development in primary than in secondary education — especially after the demise of the 11+. So for the Schools Council to be accorded a success it had to impact in some degree on the examination system. It didn't. It invented all sorts of paper plans — Ps and Qs and Fs. It laboured long and wearily towards a single system of examinations at 16. Yet none of it came to fruition. Why?

I suspect it was lack of political clout, in the widest sense of that phrase. Neither its successive Chairmen, nor its transient Secretaries, nor its more permanent officials ever saw a hard political entrepreneurial role for themselves. Reform of the English examination system has always been political job (with a small 'p'). It can only be brought to pass by someone moving easily between Oxford colleges, Whitehall corridors, Party conferences and London clubs, and fiercely articulating the case for it. The Schools Council simply never threw up anyone with the time and the skills and the drive to get on with that particular job. So the question went from committee to committee without ever really impacting on those who had to be persuaded before the politicians could come to any decision. Dr Butler and Arnold Jennings understood the problem certainly; NUT and NAS members of the Council did also. But there it stopped. So that when Shirley Williams knew the Council had come to the right decision about a common system of examinations at 16, she still appointed the Waddell Committee to try to gain greater public consent for the idea.

The major responsibility for the delay arose from Mrs Williams' assiduous procrastination — a chronic disability from which she had suffered all her political life. But more groundwork and political fixing by the Council through the bureaucracy might have made it very much more difficult for her to impose her customary delaying tactics.

The difficulty with the Schools Council was that it was so much easier to criticize than praise. This may be because in both the pre-Alex Smith reformation period and in the shorter subsequent one, the structure was never right. It always remained an uncomfortable hybrid between democratic workers' control, orchestrated by the NUT and the other teacher unions, the professional quango of the academic curriculum developers and the official advisory body to government on the curriculum and examinations. This inexplicit nature of its role was heightened by a refusal on the part of government, during the 1960s and 1970s to define in legislation the nature of its rights over either the curriculum or even the examination system. The system was made more acute by the refusal by governments of both parties to allow the fundamental advisory pillar of the 1944 Act, the Central Advisory Council, to remain in operation. Throughout its existence, neither the governance nor the role of the Schools Council was clear enough; to that extent it was always in jeopardy from a determined, right-wing government which saw the Council as an impediment to the new political 'consensus' it wished to establish in England.

But not in Scotland. There, not only have the government been spectacularly unsuccessful in establishing their new 'consensus'; but the arrangements for a consensus system for agreeing the curriculum and examinations has been an equally spectacular success. The Munn and Dunning Reports have established an agreed framework for the flexible development of the curriculum and examinations into the forseeable future. Even in Wales, there are few problems about the orderly development of a common system, since the same Board runs both examinations. The intractable problem is in England, where entrenched class conflict has always made educational consensus extremely difficult to achieve. Embroiled within that conflict, it is no wonder that the Schools Council had difficulties; probably no other quango, however organized, could have done much better.

But if the Schools Council had its faults, the material it distributed to schools did have a certain 'good housekeeping' seal of approval and was broadly trusted. An awful, empty chasm now exists. The Blin-Stoyle Curriculum Committee, cut off as it is from any responsibility for examinations, is a pale ghost of the Schools Council, and seems destined to do little more than provide tame and compliant advice to a minister who has already decided what he wants to do with the curriculum. A demoralized and surly teaching force, denied any pros-pect of promotion and with the value of their salaries eroded annually, will cease to receive the guidance it had in the past; there will be fewer outlets for those genuinely creative teachers who want to invest their spare energy in curriculum development. The price of Sir Keith Joseph's new, centralized curricular regime will not become apparent for some time; but it will be paid for in the meantime by lessons in classrooms more arid, boring and unimaginative than they need be, because the flow of ideas and assistance for those good teachers who want it has dried up.

Dr John Rae, the articulate High Master of Westminster, recently remarked that it was the public and grammar schools that got Britain

into its current economic difficulties; and it was up to these schools to
get their country out of them. It was a percipient remark. The lack of a
Schools Council, helping the curriculum forward, will tend to reinforce
a traditional grammar school curriculum and examination diet in, at any
rate, our secondary schools. It was the failure of the Schools Council to
eliminate this diet that injured the image of comprehensive education.
But the Council did something in that direction. The new prescription
(for the 'top' 60 per cent) is, apart from a few TVEI schemes which owe
a lot to previous Schools Council work, a return to that grammar school
currciculum which not only Dr Rae but also a host of other commenta-
tors insist is partly responsible for Britain's slow economic decline.
Whatever the educational virtues of that curriculum (and they are few),
it augurs no *economic* good for our nation.

For the 'bottom' 40 per cent, a new Schools Council has been
developed; it is called the Manpower Services Commission (MSC), and
its remit is to increase the technical skills of the working class, while
denying them opportunities for serious intellectual, moral and political
enrichment. The first is a worthy aspiration, but is just as necessary in
the curriculum of the so called 'top' 60 per cent. The second is, in the
longer run, doomed to failure, but will in the meantime sharpen the
class divide, widen the resentment between the privileged and the poor
of society and lessen any prospects of industrial recovery. There is some
hope that the few individuals with imagination and flair within the MSC
will sabotage its basic objectives and transform it into something more
worthy. But any such developments will be scattered and patchy. For all
the criticisms of the Humanities Project, this replacement will be worse;
whole generations of 14, 15 and 16 year olds will know that the
curriculum they are offered is designed to keep them quiet and is
unlikely to get them a job.

It is far too early to estimate how long this new, bipartite central
curricular regime will last. The danger is that it will become attractive to
politicians of both parties, which now see the curriculum, rather like the
media, as a commanding height of the cultural economy to be scaled and
held against their political enemies. So we may not see another Schools
Council for many a year yet. The hope must be that areas of agreement
will emerge where, little by little, the government will withdraw from
their central grip on the curricular and examination system and hand
back some power, not just to the teachers but to the whole community,
which, when all is said and done, has to live with the youngsters who are
educated within it.

Even with the death of the Schools Council, there is no need for
regional and even local curriculum development to cease, especially if

there is a determined local education authority or university to encourage the process. If profiles are gradually first to supplement and then replace a formal examination at 16+ (a process which the central government may not wholly set its face against) that exercise will need substantial local curricular discussion. So all is not lost. Perhaps the old Schools Council was too centralized itself, and some of the best work it was doing will survive at local level. But it remains sad that the right-wing political *putsch* which the present government has successfully achieved, should have carried away in its path a unique service to teachers in schools which, over its two decades, for all its manifest faults, did much to improve life in the classroom for many children, the morale of many of their teachers and, as such, the face of English education.

Who Killed the Schools Council?

John Mann

A Little Group of Madmen?

'It is' said Franz Joseph of his nephew's murder at Sarajevo in 1914 'the act of a little group of madmen'.[1] In this chapter I have tried to identify the little group who put paid to the Schools Council, to offer some tentative thoughts about why their task took twenty years and why in the end they were successful. Unhappily, neither the Council's founding fathers nor those who followed them really understood the price of liberty. The Council was betrayed by some of those most committed to its ideals and doubly betrayed by some who used it to achieve their own ends.

What is laughingly known as the responsible Department did little to nurture its own offspring. Many in the Department had not wanted the baby at all and were alarmed to see it so bonny.

The Founding Fathers

'I have been much impressed' wrote John Lockwood 'by the growth of a common understanding of the nature of the problem, and of a common determination to find solutions by cooperative endeavour which has characterized the meetings of the working party. The present arrangements for determining the curriculum in schools and the related examinations are not working well: in particular, teachers have insufficient scope for making or recommending modifications in the curriculum and examinations'. His Report[2] suggested a free association of equal partners, advisory to all its member interests who would retain unimpaired their right to take decisions within their own areas of responsibility. This Schools Council would control its own work and would complement existing agencies for research and development.

The Report proposed that when a preliminary study indicated the need for research or development work the Council would decide who should be approached to carry out this work. 'The results of the Council's work', said Lockwood, 'should possess only their own inherent authority'. To avoid any suspicion of central control the Council would neither publish nor approve anything in the nature of a textbook.

Lockwood then turned to staffing. The normal basis of service with the Council should be short term; a career secretariat and study team organization were not desirable. The Council would have full operational control of its staff subject only to special arrangements to protect the professional independence of HM Inspectors.

In one respect, Sir Edward Boyle's[3] acceptance of the recommendations represented a remarkable, though temporary, bouleversement. The Lockwood Committee had been appointed to resolve difficulties arising from the creation of the Curriculum Study Group. That in turn had originated in Sir David Eccles'[4] publicly-expressed view that others than teachers should be admitted to 'the secret garden of the curriculum'. Lockwood now reasserted the autonomy of schools and the new Minister accepted that assertion.

There were other unresolved questions. How was the Council to make choices if it identified needs beyond the available funds? How would it ensure that those it commissioned presented work of an appropriate quality at the time the Council needed it? By whom and on what criteria would the Council itself be judged? How was it expected to learn from its own experience? These questions had not been answered satisfactorily by 1984. There is no evidence that they were addressed at all in the early days.

What had been devised was a piece of quasi-political machinery to bring together different elements in the education service. What no-one considered sufficiently was the differing status of these representatives in their various constituencies. Nor was it ever safe to assume that all the representatives of one body shared the same assumptions and same commitment to the Council.

The Age of Disillusion

The golden 1960s passed. New approaches to management found their way to the Department of Education and Science. The Planning Branch[5] wet its toes in output budgeting and in 1968 the Fulton Report[6] recommended that the civil service as a whole should adopt either accountable management or management by objectives. In 1972 *Education: a Framework for Expansion*[7] sought to reconcile the new managerial approach and the optimism of the 1960s.

But already Britain was in an age of economic turbulence. Inflation, trade deficits, de-industrialization and unemployment provided the framework for political and economic decisions. Britain's relatively poor industrial performance was increasingly attributed to her educational deficiencies. Criticism and contraction marked the 1970s as surely as expansion and confidence had marked the 1960s.

The Department itself was not immune. Both an OECD team[8] and a House of Commons Sub-Committee[9] were sharply critical of the Department's secrecy and poor performance. This mood of disillusion affected the Schools Council too.

The Council's two paymasters, the Department of Education and Science and the Local Authority Associations, shared these feelings. In rejecting the Council's proposals for examinations at 16 and 17, the Secretary of State, Mrs Shirley Williams,[10] emphasized that the Council's work should be informed by closer knowledge of the Secretary of State's views. There was a need for 'closer engagement of the Department and the Inspectorate in the preparation of proposals and their consideration by its committees.' For their part the local authorities were to say that 'the views of other interests...have been virtually set aside' by the Council's teacher majorities.[11]

An Unhappy Conjunction

1976 saw the centenary of compulsory education,[12] the publication of a consultative document on devolution,[13] the appointment of James Hamilton as Permanent Under-Secretary at the Department of Education and Science, publication of the Yellow Paper,[14] and the first Prime Ministerial speech ever devoted wholly to education.[15] It was a most unhappy conjunction.

James Hamilton's seven-year tenure coincided almost precisely with the final phase of the Schools Council's life. His first public speech to the Association of Education Committees (AEC) outlined the Department's and his own agenda. Of the Secretary of State's duties under the 1944 Act he said:

> It must mean I believe a much closer interest by the Department in the curriculum in its widest sense, the assessment of performance and even the relationship of teaching method to perform-

ance. I have no detailed proposals to offer you today but I
believe that the so-called secret garden of the curriculum in
which the HMI already walks by professional right cannot be
allowed to remain so secret after all.[16]

When he retired in April 1984, the *Times Educational Supplement*
entitled its valedictory[17] 'The Unrepentant Centralist'. Addressing the
Association for Science Education (ASE)[18] a few weeks later, Sir James
said there was an argument for the DES acting 'more directly in certain
limited areas of curriculum'. 'In a country that has no tradition of
national initiatives on curriculum policy, I am wholly prepared' he said
'to use reforms of the exam system to bring about much needed changes
in national attitudes towards curriculum'.

Sir James' views were no doubt a major influence while he was
Permanent Under-Secretary. His appointment was a landmark in other
ways too. He was an outsider whose career had lain in aeronautical
research and development, the Department of Trade and Industry, and
the Cabinet Office. His appointment heralded other similar appointments in the Department.

Even those in the Department who represented the older tradition
were not always supportive of the Council.

The exalted mandarin who wrote the Yellow Paper[19] took a lofty
view of the Schools Council. 'The Schools Council', he said, 'has
performed moderately in commissioning development work in particular curricular areas; it has had little success in tackling examination
problems despite the availability of resources which its predecessor (the
Secondary Schools Examination Council) never had; and it has scarcely
begun to tackle the problems of the curriculum as a whole. Despite
some good quality staff work, the overall performance of the Schools
Council has in fact, both on curriculum and on examination, been
generally mediocre.' The performance of the Schools Council had been
disappointing. 'There will have to be a review of its functions and
constitution.' He emphasized also that the Department could make use
of enhanced opportunities to exercise influence over curriculum and
teaching methods.

Callaghan's Ruskin speech included only one somewhat dispara-
ging remark about the Council's recommendations on examinations:
'Maybe they haven't got it right yet'. More important, he gave Prime
Ministerial weight to the generalized criticisms of the education service
which were already widespread.

Within two or three weeks the Department had issued an 'annotated agenda'[20] in which they identified briefly 'the main educational

issues which need to be considered before the next stage'. This was the prologue to Shirley Williams' Great Debate.[21]

The clarity of her views about relations between Department and Council appeared to offer a helpful framework for the constitutional review which the Council already had in hand. Very senior officers from the Department contributed to this review and accepted its findings.

The New Look

The Secretary of State had made it clear that she wanted to end the overall teacher majority in Council committees.[22] She wanted a smaller Governing Council, greater lay participation and a significant number of members appointed in virtue of their individual qualities and experience by the Secretary of State on a personal basis. It was never clear how or by whom the performance of members appointed in this way would ever be assessed. But then the Department is not strong in stating its criteria and to this day no-one knows in what respects the Council's performance up to 1976 was mediocre or who it disappointed.

1977 was a year of frenzied activity which culminated on 31 January 1978 in a meeting of the Governing Council at which Sir Alex Smith presented a new constitution. Like the états-généraux of pre-revolutionary France the Council was to have three major estates: pay-masters, teachers and laity. But whereas the états-généraux had one Chamber for each estate, the Schools Council had a different balance of representation in each of its three main committees: Finance and Priorities, Professional and Convocation. These three were supported by a complex matrix of subordinate committees: the Committee for Wales dealt with matters in one region, the Primary and Secondary Committees with different phases of education, the Examinations Committee with one function, and the Publications Company with another. There were Liaison Committees linking Convocation with parents, higher and further education, and the world of industry and commerce. The new Council also acknowledged that there was a need for subject committees to represent the special expertise and needs of each major area of the curriculum. Despite the elaboration of this matrix, when in due course the new Council announced new pro-grammes of work it found that these did not correspond with any of its existing committees. New monitoring and review groups were therefore appointed to oversee four of the five new programmes.

This elaborate committee system had some virtues. A great many people were drawn into some aspect of the Council's work and some had a fairly extended view of the Council arising from their service on several committees. But it had other disadvantages. Members of the major committees were members of the Council but it was never clear whether a member of a subject committee or a project advisory group was a member or not. Unhappily, the constitution ensured that only the Chairman and perhaps six or eight others could have an overall view of the Council's policies and work. For many committee members the Council had no corporate existence beyond the intermittent meetings they attended.

There was a more serious problem. Beyond the cost of travel and subsistence, servicing so large a number of committees required a great administrative effort and a large secretariat. These costs would have been supportable had there been sufficient work. As the Council itself said[23] in its evidence to Mrs Trenaman there was a case for having a limited number of groups to look at particular areas of the curriculum or particular stages of education. But it was hardly necessary to keep all areas and stages under review at all times. Within the Council's limited budget it was not even possible to allow each committee to produce subject or stage bulletins whenever it wished. We had neither staff nor money to do this.

Another source of frustration was the complex relationship between the major committees. As Sir Alex Smith had said 'a different power lies within each of the committees. None will be able to ignore the views of the others.'[24] Few inside the Council, and hardly any outside, were able to unravel this mystery. The constitutional requirement for committees to consult each other added greatly to the weight of administrative work.

Let no-one be in doubt. The vision of 1978 was both a noble and a subtle one. The constitution of 1978 was a notable attempt to represent the complex organic relationships of education and society. But the search for this chimera diverted the intellectuals from the more pressing need for an efficient machine.

For all that, the Department's leading representative on the Schools Council, Deputy Secretary John Hudson, welcomed the Report. 'The proposals represented a compromise in which no party had gained all that it might have wished; the Department's view was that the proposals should be accepted and made to work as well as possible.... The DES will', he said, 'support the proposals as they stand'.[25] Whether all his colleagues shared this commitment or even knew of it is hard to credit.

What is odd about the Department's involvement in the review is that they were content to rearrange deckchairs. The review was concerned only with the Council's committee structure and membership. The Schools Council's place in the education system was not in question. Its object and powers remained the same. 'The object of the Schools Council shall be the promotion of education by carrying out research into and keeping under review the curricula, teaching methods and examinations in schools, including the organization of schools so far as it affects their curricula.'[26]

Another thing which went unchanged was the Council's independent status. For many years the foreword to its annual reports[27] began 'The Schools Council for Curriculum and Examinations is an independent body . . .', a charitable trust. Both the breadth of its object and its declared independence might have been challenged. In spite of Mrs Williams' letter they were not and John Hudson stood up promptly to declare departmental support for the new constitution.

The Department's commitment was further emphasized when John Hudson and Sheila Browne, the Senior Chief Inspector, formed part of the panel to interview candidates for the new post of Secretary to the Council. The successful candidate's letter of application[28] concluded, 'There is a feeling abroad that power in the English schools system is not so much distributed among the various partners as fragmented. The Schools Council's new constitution seems to offer a way of making the partnership effective. I should therefore welcome the opportunity of helping the Council to take the lead in developing education.' No-one on the panel even mentioned these bold aspirations. It seemed reasonable to conclude that they had at least the tacit assent of all the parties represented on that panel.

If the new Secretary had high ambitions, so too had the new Chairman. John Tomlinson has said 'A serious flaw in the constitution of the Mark I Council had been a refusal to permit it a place in teacher training. I made it a condition of my accepting appointment as Chairman that this should not continue to be the case.'[29] Even more significant was his keynote address to the new Convocation. 'I wonder', he said, 'if historians will say of our efforts that they justified the intention and the hope of enabling constructive public debate of big educational issues after the sharp but possibly superficial disagreements of recent times. Shall we be seen as this generation's educational monument — alongside 1902, 1918 and 1944?'[30] Heady words indeed, but well within the terms of the Council's constitution.

A Change of Government

The return of a Conservative government in May 1979 constituted a new threat. The new Secretary of State, Mark Carlisle, began an immediate review of educational advisory bodies. But the Schools Council, he said, had been recently re-structured and clearly had a role to play.[31] But 'Mr Carlisle's opinion of the Schools Council will, alas, count for little when the axe falls. ... He will not be the man though to decide the Council's fate. That, the Review knows, is already in the hands of a caucus of senior civil servants and non-Cabinet advisers who owe the Council no loyalty.'[32]

For the time being, the Council seemed to flourish. A good many ministerial speeches[33] referred to the Council in relatively warm terms. In March 1981 *The School Curriculum*[34] referred to the Council's work on records of achievement, curriculum development, and links between schools and industry. The Central Office of Information suggested that other government departments should use the Schools Council's expertise if they wished to develop teaching materials.[35] The Central Policy Review Staff recommended building on the work of the Schools Council[36] and so too did the Manpower Services Commission.[37] Professor Meredydd G. Hughes recommended that the proposed schools management unit should be established within the Schools Council.[38]

The Yellow Paper had complained that the Council had scarcely begun to tackle the problems of the curriculum as a whole, and in *The Practical Curriculum*[39] it tried to do this. The Council worked furiously to have *The Practical Curriculum* ready for publication early in 1981 so that it followed soon after the Department's *The School Curriculum*. The Schools Council was ready first but the Department insisted that the Schools Council's publication be held back.

Above all, in 1981 the reconstituted Schools Council survived its major test. In March Mrs Nancy Trenaman, Principal of St Anne's College, Oxford, was invited to conduct the review suggested by Pliatsky.[40] Her main conclusion was that 'the Schools Council should continue and with its present functions'.[41] Unhappily, the report commissioned by Mark Carlisle was delivered to his successor. John Tomlinson had already said that he must shortly leave the Chair and no-one at the Council was ever to establish the rapport with Sir Keith which John Tomlinson had enjoyed with his predecessor.

The Department and the Council

In fourteen years the Council had thirteen Joint Secretaries. Apart from a handful of Editors, one or two Information Officers and a few Curriculum and Research Officers, the Council had no directly recruited or permanent staff until 1978. Clearly, those responsible for staffing the Council like this had little regard for team building, expertise in the Council's affairs, the ability of organizations to learn from experience, or the need to see things through to a successful conclusion. For its part, the Department of Education and Science seems to have moved people to and from the Council as and when it chose. A surprisingly high proportion seem to have been long-serving officers within two or three years of retirement.

In July 1982 I wrote:

> Three heads of our committee secretariat have spanned a little more than four years and we lost a second finance officer only two years after I joined the Council. They were both fine men but neither had held a finance post before coming to the Council and neither had accountancy qualifications. For fifteen years the Department allowed the Council to develop a new support system for educational development involving complex contracts with many other bodies without ensuring that the Council had the capacity to develop and run appropriate financial systems. Even in 1978 and 1979 it was I who had to press for a qualified accountant and we were only able to recruit one in 1980.[42]

Most serious was the apparent lack of communication between different branches of the Department. John Hudson seemed to have given full support to the review findings and the decision to appoint a single Secretary. That appointment clearly had implications for the structure of other posts.

Most urgent was the need to introduce a pension scheme for Council staff. This depended on the findings of a departmental inspection team that had to satisfy itself that posts were appropriately graded. Between my appointment in June 1978 and actually starting work in October, I made two special visits to the Department to discuss the inspection report. At the second meeting on 22 September I was told that the draft report would be ready in about six weeks and we discussed arrangements for consulting staff about the draft. We even discussed arrangements for submitting the agreed report to Council committees. What actually happened was quite different. We received no draft report. The team came to see us on 4 December. They brought no draft but we were led to expect it early in January. It did not arrive. An interim note of some key recommendations arrived too late for me to consult staff before submitting the recommendations to a major committee in January. As March approached it became clear that we would not have the report in time to submit it to the Finance and Priorities Committee in March. Dated 1979, the report eventually reached me on 7 March 1980, two years after the new constitution came into effect.

Of course some points of detail had been settled and a very senior officer indeed had been to see me in February 1979 to explain that he and his closest colleague were in the fast stream and, if there were any difficulties with his slower subordinates, I had only to have a word and particular matters could be quickly sorted.

My experience of the Department's inspection team was my first direct involvement with the Department. Instead of making rapid progress in the creation of a new management team the Council had to proceed piecemeal until a new team finally gathered during the course of the Trenaman review in 1981. Other difficulties arose from the Department's membership of the Council. The constitutional device adopted in 1978 to meet Mrs Williams' wish that the Council should be more responsive to the Secretary of State's wishes was to include departmental officers and HMI in all the Council's major committees. Eight of the twenty-eight members of the Finance and Priorities Committee were to be appointed by the Secretaries of State for Education and Science and for Wales and eight by the local authority associations. Some of the Secretary of State's representatives seemed to find it incongruous and others frustrating that in committee their reasoning sometimes failed to win assent though they clearly regarded the Council as some sort of departmental fief. Many of the other members were experienced local authority politicians, local authority officials, or trade union officials appointed or elected, all well-versed in some of the robuster kinds of public debate. Some of those without this experience carried little conviction in Council committees.

The difficulty the Department's officers had in working as members of Council committees is well illustrated by a letter dated 2 July 1981 from Miss Dawson, 'I understand that Mr Ulrich deliberately withheld DES *approval*'[43] to the Council's annual report at Convocation. My reply, never acknowledged, said, 'As I understand the constitutional position, it is for Convocation acting corporately to approve the annual report rather than the constituent members acting separately'.[44]

The Department never recognized the Council's status as a charitable body nor its need to be seen to be independent if it was to be a credible change agent. In my first few months at the Council I had to refute in almost equal numbers the charges that I was a mere lackey of the Department or the tool of the National Union of Teachers.

Similar issues had already arisen twice in 1981. In discussing the publication of *The Practical Curriculum* and *The School Curriculum* with Philip Halsey[45] I had had to make it clear that it was for the Chairman, or perhaps a committee, rather than for me as the Council's officer, to delay a Council publication in deference to the Department. Similar difficulties arose from the Parents Liaison Committee's wish to publish advice about home-school communication. The Liaison Committee believed that schools ought to publish more information than that required by regulations issued under the 1980 Education Act. But they took the view that it would be harmful to do as the regulations required and publish external examination results. To the evident annoyance of departmental officers, the Liaison Committee's views were endorsed by Professional Committee and Convocation. What the Council published in June 1981 was therefore a list of the statutory requirements recommended by the Council and other information recommended by the Council with a note as to where to find the full list of statutory requirements.[46]

It was doubtless incidents like these which led Wally Ulrich in his evidence to Mrs Trenaman on 30 July and 3 August 1981 to say that 'the Council required a competent, loyal and submissive staff'.[47] With experience of working for half a dozen public bodies, I can say with some confidence that the Council's staff were as competent as any and outstandingly loyal to the Council. One would hardly expect professional people of stature to be submissive, but we might perhaps have learned to respect the Department's senior officers more had we seen a little more of them. Some had the good fortune to meet and hear Wally Ulrich at one of the three meetings of Convocation he was able to attend at a London hotel and he was once able to pay a fleeting visit to the Council itself. On the strength of this experience he gave extensive evidence to Mrs Trenaman. Though he remained ultimately responsible, the Council saw nothing of him after the meeting of Convocation on 30 June 1981. Similarly, in his own seven years at the Department, Sir James Hamilton managed one three-hour visit to the Council.

What was perhaps even more interesting about the Department's evidence to Mrs Trenaman was that the Department now rejected the commitment John Hudson had expressed. The departmental brief[48] criticized the lack of a board of management, the tripartite structure of the main committees, the balance of membership on Finance and Priorities and Professional committees, the lack of clarity about the relative function of Finance and Priorities and Professional committees, the concentration by subject committees on their own subject, the size of the main committees, and the absence of any restriction on the length of time for which a member might serve. For the most part changes to meet these criticisms would have been sensible improvements but, given the Department's long experience, it must surely have been aware of issues like these during the review. It is hardly sufficient for DES officials to say 'that the internal nature of that review had precluded very radical proposals'.[49]

What they went on to say was much more significant: 'In any case the DES stance in relation to curriculum issues had changed substantially since then. It was now accepted generally that the Department could speak with authority on curriculum issues and present Ministers were perhaps more inclined to look for radical changes.' How the Deparment must have relished the September Cabinet reshuffle.

Sir Keith Takes Over

Behind an apparent taste for inconclusive armchair analysis lay Britain's most incisive and interventionist post-war Minister of Education. While some of his fellow ministers talked quite openly of 'the general failure of the public education system',[50] Sir Keith Joseph strode boldly in the secret garden. Among his first tasks was to receive Mrs Trenaman's review of the Schools Council. 'We have weighed carefully the available evidence including of course Mrs Trenaman's report' he wrote[51] to the Council's Acting Chairman, Dr Peter Andrews, and might have added in plain words that he totally rejected Mrs Trenaman's assessment. But of course Sir Keith had access to some 'evidence' that Mrs Trenaman never saw. 'We must have some ritual bloodletting', said his junior minister Rhodes Boyson.[52] The Prime Minister herself bandied words with a former Council officer: 'The Schools Council always was a lousy organization'.[53]

Could the Council have been Saved?

The Council does not stand alone. It is one of many bodies to have been subjected to rigorous examination since Mrs Thatcher took office in 1979. The Centre for Educational Disadvantage and the Advisory Council for Adult and Continuing Education have been dispatched. The Social Science Research Council, HM Inspectorate, the Centre for Information on Language Teaching, and now the Council for National Academic Awards have been subjected to scrutiny. Non-conforming chairmen of area health authorities have been sacked and the metropolitan authorities are to be abolished. The odds seem somewhat against the government countenancing the existence of an independent Schools Council.

But could the council have done more to save itself? Its many friends gave voluminous evidence to Mrs Trenaman and in the following year the Department was taken aback by the protests against Sir Keith's decision to disband the Council. The weight of this support is surprising because the Council had not set out to win friends. In my own time, at least half a dozen distinguished and enthusiastic project directors crossed swords with the Council about the publication of their chef d'oeuvres. Radicals were often disappointed by the Council's failure to espouse their causes and innovators by the Council's inability to deliver support. Others were equally put out by the Council's support for what seemed to be radical and trendy developments in, for example, health and social education. Nor had the Council won extensive support among practising teachers. Though its royalties were running at £250,000 a year, the Council used many different publishers and had no distinctive house style. Many teachers who use or adapt its materials are unaware of their connection with the Council.

Conclusion

An unworkable dream? No! The Council needed an engine room to match its superstructure. The crew needed radar to pick out rocks and shoals. But there was no way of evading the Exocet designed by Hamilton and built by Joseph.

There is no doubt who the killers were. How long it took them, and at what unnecessary cost, is material for another chapter.

Notes

1 Quoted in a report presented to the Preliminary Peace Conference (1919), Commission on War Guilt.
2 Ministry of Education (1964) *Report of the Working Party on the Schools' Curricula and Examinations*, (the Lockwood Committee), London, HMSO.
3 SIR EDWARD BOYLE, Minister of Education, 1962–64.
4 Sir DAVID ECCLES, Minister of Education, 1959–62.
5 (1970) EPP No 1, London, HMSO.
6 (1968) Fulton Report on the Civil Service, London HMSO.
7 Department of Education and Science (1972) *Education: a Framework for Expansion*, Cmnd 5174, London HMSO.

8 (1975) Educational Development Strategy in England and Wales, OECD.
9 (1976) Expenditure Committee of House of Commons; Education Arts and Home Office Sub Committee.
10 Mrs Shirley Williams, Secretary of State for Education and Science, 1976–79.
11 (1977) *Officers Report to the AMA and ACC Education Committees.*
12 Sandon's Education Art of 1876.
13 Office of the Lord President of the Council (1976) *Devolution: the English Dimension,* London, HMSO.
14 Secretary of State for Education and Science (1976) *School Education in England: Problems and Initiatives,* July.
15 The Ruskin Speech, Rt. Hon. James Callaghan, 18 October 1976.
16 *The Teacher,* 2 July 1976.
17 *The Times Educational Supplement,* 29 April 1983.
18 *Education in Science* No. 103, June 1983.
19 Secretary of State for Education and Science (1976) *op. cit.*
20 Department of Education and Science (1976) 'Annotated Agenda', November.
21 'Great Debate' — a series of regional conferences organized by the Department of Education and Science, February and March 1977.
22 Department of Education and Science (1977) *The Schools Council,* paper submitted to Schools Council Review Body, January.
23 What future does the Review Group see for the subject committees, SC 81/290, *Finance and Priorities Committee,* 21 July 1981.
24 *Governing Council,* 31 January 1978.
25 *Ibid.*
26 (1978) *Constitution of the Schools Council for Curriculum and Examinations,* 1 September 1978.
27 Certainly from 1969–70 to 1977–78.
28 J. MANN to D.H. ALLEN, 26 May 1978.
29 TOMLINSON, J.G.R. (1981) *The Schools Council: A Chairman's Salute and Envoi.* Address to British Association for the Advancement of Science, 1 September.
30 TOMLINSON, J.G.R. (1978) *Address to Convocation,* 14 November.
31 Secretary of State to National Association of Head Teachers, 29 May 1979.
32 *The Weekly Education Review,* 14 June 1979.
33 For example, Minister of State, Lady Young to SEO, 6 July 1979; Mr Neil Macfarlane Parliamentary Under-Secretary, to BACIE, 26 September 1979; Secretary of State to press conference on I level and 17+, 14 October 1980; Mr Neil Macfarlane Parliamentary Under-Secretary, to ASE, 4 April 1981.
34 Department of Education and Science (1981) *The School Curriculum,* London, HMSO.
35 By letter to Secretary of Schools Council, 4 September 1979 and by letter to DES, 18 June 1980.
36 Central Policy Review Staff (1980) *Education Training and Industrial Performance.*
37 Manpower Services Commission (1981) *Manpower Review.*
38 HUGHES, M.G. (1981) *Professional Development for Senior Staff in Schools and Colleges,* report comissioned by the DES, October 1981.

39 Schools Council (1981) *The Practical Curriculum.*
40 Department of Educational Science (1980) *Report on Non-Departmental Public Bodies*, Cmnd. 7797.
41 Department of Education and Science (1981) *Review of the Schools Council*, October 1981.
42 TOMLINSON, J.G.R. (1982) in *Education*, 23 July.
43 Miss D.J. DAWSON to KEITH McWILLIAMS, Deputy Secretary of Schools Council, 2 July 1981.
44 J. MANN to Miss D.J. DAWSON, 10 July 1981.
45 At that time Under-Secretary, Department of Education and Science.
46 Schools Council (1981) *Home School Communication*, June.
47 Notes of the meeting with DES officials on Thursday 30 July and Monday 3 August 1981. Circulated to all members of the Schools Council following a request at the Professional Committee on 15 June 1982.
48 Review of the Schools Council: Aide-Memoire for DES Witnesses, no date.
49 Notes of a meeting with DES Officials, 30 July and 3 August 1981.
50 I heard a junior minister use precisely these words in 1982.
51 22 April 1982.
52 To SEO delegation, summer 1981.
53 Private conversation with a former Joint Secretary of the Schools Council.

Notes on Contributors

Eric Briault, CBE, was involved with the Schools Council from its earliest days, serving on several of its committees. He chaired the Second Sixth Form Working Party which produced a blueprint for 16–19 education and examinations. He was Education Officer for the Inner London Education Authority.

Geoffrey Cockerill was seconded from the Department of Education and Science as Joint Secretary to the Schools Council from November 1970 to June 1972. He had been Secretary to the Public Schools Commission, and subsequently became Secretary to the University Grants Committee. He is now retired.

Don Cooper joined the Schools Council as a Field Officer in 1976, having previously been Principal of Cromwell Community College, Chatteris, Cambridgeshire. He became Director of the Council's *Programme Two* (helping individual teachers to become more effective) in 1979, and remained with the Council until its closure. He is currently directing the dissemination of three of the Programme Two activities.

Joan Dean was a member of the Professional Committee from 1978 representing the National Association of Inspectors and Educational Advisers. She was on the planning group for Programme Four, dealing with the needs of individual children, and a member of the Monitoring Group for Programme Two, helping teachers to become more effective. She was also a member of the working party which produced *Primary Practice*. She is Chief Inspector for the Surrey Local Education Authority.

Alan Evans was a member of the Schools Council Committee for Wales from 1970–83; he was Chairman of its Secondary Sub-committee from 1975. He is Secretary to the National Union of Teachers' Education Committee.

Arnold Jennings, CBE, was Headmaster of secondary schools for twenty-five years; a member of the National Union of Teachers' Executive and Chairman of the NUT's Secondary Advisory Committee; President of the Headmasters' Association (1977) and the Joint Association of Classical Teachers. He was a member of the Secondary Schools Examinations Council (1961–64) and then a member of the Schools Council through the whole of its life, and was Acting Chairman at its demise. He chaired the Classics Committee, Steering Committee C and the Examinations Committee, was a member of the Programme Committee, then Professional and Finance and Priorities Committees. He is now in busy retirement.

John Mann was the first, and only, Permanent Secretary to the Schools Council (October 1978–October 1983). He had been Deputy Education Officer Sheffield, and went on to be Director of Education, London Borough of Harrow. He was largely responsible for writing both *The Practical Curriculum* and *Primary Practice*.

Maurice Plaskow was a member of the Humanities Project team (1967–70) then joined the Schools Council staff where he was a Curriculum Officer until he took early retirement on closure of the Council in 1984.

Christopher Price was a close observer of the Council as ministerial Parliamentary Private Secretary, educational journalist and TV commentator, and chaired the Select Committee on Education, Science and the Arts. He taught for ten years before entering Parliament. His first head became a Joint Secretary, his second the last Council Chairman.

Margaret Raff was a member of the Council's Secondary Curriculum Committee, and served on a number of other committees and working groups. She teaches at Regents Park School, Southampton, where she has been involved in the Council's Skills for Working Life Project.

Jean Rudduck was a research officer at the Council and worked on *Enquiry 1*. She became a member of the Humanities Project, and went to be Assistant Director to Lawrence Stenhouse at the Centre for Applied Research in Education, University of East Anglia, where she directed several Council (and other) projects. She is now Professor of Education at the University of Sheffield.

Sir Alex Smith was Chairman of the Schools Council (1975–78) during the critical constitutional review. He was at the time Director of Manchester Polytechnic. He is now a business consultant.

Freddie Sparrow taught for twenty years, then did research in a university for four years, before becoming involved with the Schools Council, and became a member of its research staff in 1967. He was Chief Research Officer until he retired in 1980.

John Tomlinson, CBE, was Chairman of the Schools Council from April 1978 to December 1981, a period which saw the emergence of *Principles and Programmes*, and the Trenaman enquiry. He was always convinced that the Council was a most effective body, both for thinking and acting, containing a proper balance of politicians, professionals and community representatives. He is now Director of the Institute of Education, University of Warwick, having been Chief Education Officer for Cheshire 1971–1985.

Jack Wrigley, CBE, was a member of the Curriculum Study Group, before the establishment of the Schools Council, where he became Director of Studies (1966–75). He is Professor of Education at the University of Reading.